U1020061

汉语口语教程

第三册

北京语言大学出版社
BEIJING LANGUAGE AND CULTURE
UNIVERSITY PRESS

图书在版编目（CIP）数据

汉语口语教程．第三册 / 杨寄洲，贾永芬编著．--
北京：北京语言大学出版社，2022.11
ISBN 978-7-5619-6179-7

Ⅰ.①汉… Ⅱ.①杨… ②贾… Ⅲ.①汉语－口语－
对外汉语教学－教材 Ⅳ.① H195.4

中国版本图书馆 CIP 数据核字 (2022) 第 199261 号

汉语口语教程 第三册

HANYU KOUYU JIAOCHENG DI-SAN CE

责任编辑：王巧燕　李金梅
排版制作：北京创艺涵文化发展有限公司
责任印制：周　燚

出版发行：北京语言大学出版社
社　　址：北京市海淀区学院路 15 号，100083
网　　址：www.blcup.com
电子信箱：service@blcup.com
电　　话：编 辑 部　8610-82303647/3592/3724
　　　　　国内发行　8610-82303650/3591/3648
　　　　　海外发行　8610-82303365/3080/3668
　　　　　北语书店　8610-82303653
　　　　　网购咨询　8610-82303908
印　　刷：北京鑫丰华彩印有限公司

版　　次：2022 年 11 月第 1 版　　印　　次：2022 年 11 月第 1 次印刷
开　　本：787 毫米 × 1092 毫米　1/16　　印　　张：12.5
字　　数：199 千字
定　　价：55.00 元

PRINTED IN CHINA
凡有印装质量问题，本社负责调换。QQ：1367565611，电话：010-82303590

前言

《汉语口语教程》是为零起点的汉语学习者编写的，适用于开展学历教育和非学历教育以及各类国际汉语教育的教学单位。

本教程的编写理念是：力求培养学生成才。

选择学习汉语的外国学生，尤其是来华学习汉语的留学生大多处于人生的最佳年龄段，他们万里迢迢来到中国，来到我们身边，追求自己的人生梦想，跟我们学习汉语，我们不能辜负了他们。我们一定要树立培养学生成才的理念，哪怕学生只学一年半载，也要为他们今后的发展着想。

口语课是单项技能训练课。

如果说听力课和阅读课重在输入的话，那么口语课则重在输出。这就要求学生在课堂上要尽可能多地开口说话，要求教师要借助教材，调动和利用一切教学手段和技巧，激发学生的表达欲望。师生之间、生生之间要开展接近实际的交际会话，培养、操练学生的口头表达能力。要让学生通过一年的学习，能够运用汉语满足日常交际需要，并为他们升入高年级或进入其他专业学习（如学医、学工等）打下一个良好的基础。

口语课堂应是师生互动、演示教材的"剧场"。

我们希望，任课教师一定要充分利用课堂，充分利用师生面对面的语境，指导并共同进行师生之间、生生之间的交际会话。课堂交际会话当然是模拟实际生活的会话，尽管如此，这四五十分钟的一节课，对于学生来说都弥足珍贵。我们建议教师不要过多地使用PPT，您面对学生真诚坦然的微笑，亲切悦耳的话语，声情并茂的讲解与朗读，与学生面对面、心与心的交流，这是任何教材、任何课件都无法代替的。

口语课堂上，教师和学生都要动起来。再好的教材都是死的。语言是交际的工具，是最灵动、最活泼、最实用的。尤其是初级阶段，学生能不能尽快用汉语进行最实用的交际，对他们影响巨大而深远。

口语应是带表情的动与说的结合。所以建议教师活用教材，把课堂当成"剧场"，把教材当成"剧本"，教师当好导演，学生当好演员，师生互动，把每节课都演成一幕话剧。

本教程分 4 册共 64 课，供零起点的汉语学习者使用 1 年。4 册书共出生词约 2000 个，多为常用词。

鉴于各个教学单位口语课的课时不统一，有多有少。所以，完全可以从本单位的实际出发，从教学对象的实际出发，灵活使用本教程。

编写体例

一、课文

本教程的课文多是情景会话。情景设计都基于来华留学生的学习和生活。编者的意图是，学习和练习这些会话，使学习者能熟练地运用它们，满足日常学习和生活的交际需要。

为了尽早培养学生的成段表达能力，本教程从第一册第10课起，就设置了一个“读后说”的练习项目。其内容都是一些小短文。

课文是重中之重！

课堂上教师要集中精力，用大量时间带领学生把课文读熟。教师要大声示范朗读、大声领读；同时，要求学生大声跟读、大声齐读、大声地单独朗读。

朗读是口语课堂教学和课外练习的主要方法。要鼓励学生大声地、反复地朗读，让学生通过朗读感受汉语的语音语调和语气，领略汉语的语言美。不论是会话课文还是叙述短文，都要求学生最少要朗读十遍以上，达到熟读成诵的程度。这样，也只有这样，用的时候才能脱口而出。

通过一年的训练，大多数学生的口语能力应能基本满足日常学习和生活的交际需要。这是被多年教学实践证明了的。

第一、二册（1～32课）的课文都配有汉语拼音，同时提供英文译文供学生参考，拼音是为了减少学生朗读的困难，英文译文是为了减少学生理解的困难。我们的教学对象大多都具有高中以上学历，尽管英语不一定是每个学生的母语，但本教程的内容都是基础的日常会话，英文译文对他们理解课文应该有所帮助。

第三、四册（33～64课）除了生词加注拼音和英文释义外，课文不再加注拼音，也不再提供英文译文。

效果如何，要由教学实践来检验。我们希望听到一线教师的意见和建议，以便及时修正。

二、生词

本教程每课的生词部分都有拼音和英文释义。

三、注释

口语课堂教学没有讲练语法的任务，因此，本教程的注释只是对课文中出现的一些语法点或重点词语的用法加以简要的说明，为教师教学提供一些方便。例句可供学习者参考。

四、练习

口语课重在培养学生“说”的言语技能，但听说读写这四项言语技能既相对独立又相互依存，既相互制约又相互促进。听不懂，一定不会说；读不懂，也一定影响说。没有大量的输入，不可能有理想的输出。因此，口语课要达到预期的效果，必须充分利用各项言语技能的相互促进作用，通过有效的输入，激发表达欲望，促进齿舌运动，使学习者发出正确的汉语语音语调，说出正确的有交际意义的句子，从而达到日常学习和生活想要达到的交际目的。

本教程通用的练习是：朗读并分辨近音字词的语音语调、替换、选词填空、完成句子或会话并大声朗读、结合自身实际回答问题等。

口语课必须重视语音语调的训练。因此，本教程始终把语音语调的练习放在非常重要的位置。教材在这方面的努力，也是为教学做个提示：要想让学生说一口正确的汉语普通话，教师的作用是教材无法代替的。

练习要求学生课外完成，教师可及时检查和纠正，以提高学生的学习质量。

练习不仅是复练课堂所学，同时希望学生能够通过做练习，培养自学能力。严格地说，没有自学能力的学生不可能成才。在网络时代，只要想学、爱学，随时都可以学习。要引导学生刻苦自学、努力成才。所以，本教程在练习中一再提示，遇到不懂的词语、不懂的文化知识点，要去问百度、问谷歌，要随手去查电子词典——它们都是课外的“老师”。教师要鼓励学生自学，帮助学生培养良好的学习习惯。

在初级阶段，受词汇、语法的制约，会话课文都是情景会话。情景会话就必然受情景的限定。为了弥补初级口语会话的不足，我们在每课练习部分的最后，添加了一个“怎么表达”，这实际就是交际会话。一般说来，交际会话的句子和会话不太受情景的制约。需要说明的是，这也不属于课堂教学的内容，而是为学生自学准备的。

练习中的诗词和著名词句都是学生自学的内容。出诗词的目的是想利用其合辙押韵的特点，培养学生的朗读兴趣，同时也为他们今后的深造奠定基础。一些我们耳熟能详的词句，让学生接触一下，不无益处。

本教程的编写得到业内朋友的指导和帮助，北京语言大学出版社也给予大力支持，在此表示衷心的感谢。

编者

2019 年 6 月

Preface

Spoken Chinese Course is written for Chinese beginners. It is suitable for the academic institutions developing credential or non-credential education, as well as teaching Chinese for speakers of other languages.

The compiling idea of this course is to strive to cultivate students' talents.

The foreign students who choose to study Chinese, especially those who come to China to study Chinese, are at their best ages in life. They come all the way to China, to us, to pursue their dreams of life and learn Chinese with us, thus we can't let them down. We must hold the belief to cultivate students' talents. Even if they just study for a year or so, we should consider their future development.

The oral class is a single-skill training course.

While the listening and reading classes focus on input, the oral class stresses output. Therefore, students are required to speak as much as possible in class, and teachers are required to stimulate students' desire to express themselves adopting all kinds of teaching methods and techniques by the aid of the coursebook. Genuine conversations should take place between the teacher and students, as well as among students, in order to develop and train students' oral expression ability. After one year's study, students should be able to have daily communication in Chinese, and lay a solid foundation for their further study in higher grades or other majors (e.g. medicine, engineering, etc.).

The oral class should be a theater for the teacher to interact with students and demonstrate the coursebook.

We hope that the teacher can make full use of the class and the face-to-face context between him/her and students to guide and make teacher-student and student-student conversations. Classroom conversation is of course a conversation that stimulates real life. Nevertheless, the 40- to 50-minute lesson is especially valuable for students. We suggest teachers to try not to use PPT too much. Your sincere and calm smile, kind and sweet words, remarkable explanation and reading aloud, and your face-to-face and heart-to-heart communication with students cannot be replaced by any coursebook or courseware.

In the oral Chinese class, both the teacher and students should be active. No matter how good the coursebook is, it is rigid. Language is the tool of communication. It is the most intelligent, active and practical. Especially in the primary stage, whether students can use Chinese to communicate as soon as possible has a huge and far-reaching impact on them.

Spoken language should be a combination of expressive movement and speech. So teachers are advised to make flexible use of the coursebook. Teachers should take the classroom as a theater and the coursebook as the play script. The teacher should act as the director, while students should act as actors and actresses. They should interact with each other to put on a play in each class.

This course contains four books with 64 lessons. It is suitable for Chinese beginners and can be used for one year. There are about 2,000 new words in the four books, most of which are common words.

Since the hours for the oral class vary in each institution, you can use this coursebook flexibly according to the actual conditions of your institution and your students.

Compiling style:

I. Texts

The texts in this coursebook are mostly situation conversations. The situations are based on the study and life of foreign students in China. The compilers aim to make students learn and practice these conversations so as to use them proficiently and meet their communicative needs in study and life.

In order to develop students' ability to express themselves in paragraph as early as possible, a "speaking after reading" part is designed from Lesson 10 of Book 1. All the texts in this part are short essays.

Texts are the most important!

In class, the teacher should focus on texts and spend much time to lead students to read texts fluently. The teacher should model reading aloud and ask students to follow, and read aloud together and individually.

Reading aloud is the main method of oral classroom teaching and extracurricular practice. Encourage students to read aloud and repeatedly. Let students perceive the pronunciation, intonation and tones of Chinese and the beauty of Chinese by reading aloud.

Whether it is a conversation text or a narrative essay, the teacher should require students to read it aloud for at least ten times to reach the level of reciting it. In this way, and only in this way, can students blurt it out when using it.

Through one year's training, most students should be able to communicate in their daily study and life. This has been proved by years of teaching practice.

Pinyin and English translation for the texts are provided in Books 1 and 2 (Lessons 1-32). (To save space, the English translation is provided as an online resource for teachers and students to download if needed.) The pinyin is added to make it easier for students to read the texts aloud, and the English translation is provided to reduce students' difficulty in understanding. Most of our students have a senior high school education or above. Although English is not necessarily every student's first language, all the content of this coursebook is basic daily conversations, and the English translation should be helpful for them to understand the texts.

In Books 3 and 4 (Lessons 33-64), except for the pinyin and English definition for the new words, no pinyin and English translation for the texts are provided. The effect will be tested by the teaching practice. We hope to hear the opinions and suggestions from the teachers, so as to make timely revisions.

II. New Words

The pinyin and English definition are provided for the new words in each lesson in the coursebook.

III. Notes

Grammar is not taught and practiced in the oral class. Therefore, the notes in this coursebook are only brief explanations of some grammatical points or key words and expressions that appear in the texts, to provide convenience for teaching. Example sentences are for students' reference.

IV. Exercises

Oral class focuses on developing students' speaking skills. However, the four language skills of listening, speaking, reading and writing are relatively independent on one hand, but dependent on each other on the other hand. If you don't understand what was said, you can't speak. If you don't understand what was written, your speaking skills will also be affected. Without a large amount of input, it is impossible to have ideal output. Therefore, to achieve the expected effect in oral class, we must make full use of the mutual promotion of various language skills. Through effective input, the desire to express is stimulated, and the tongue and teeth movements are promoted. Students are able to produce correct pronunciation and intonation of Chinese, and say the correct sentences with communicative meanings, so as to achieve the communicative purpose needed in daily study and life.

The common exercises in this coursebook include reading aloud and distinguishing the pronunciation and intonation of similar words, substitution, choosing words to fill in the blanks, completing the sentences or conversations and reading them aloud, and answering the questions according to the students' actual situations.

The training of pronunciation and intonation is very important in oral class. Therefore, this coursebook always attaches great importance to the pronunciation and intonation exercises. The effort of the coursebook in this regard is also a reminder for teaching: to make students speak Mandarin correctly, the role of teachers cannot be replaced by coursebooks.

Students are required to finish the exercises after class. Teachers can check and correct them in time to improve the quality of students' study.

The exercises are designed not only to practice what students have learned in class, but also to train students' self-study ability. Strictly speaking, students without self-study ability can't be successful. In the Internet age, as long as you want to and love to learn, you can learn at any time. Teachers should guide students to study hard independently and become successful. Therefore, the course in the exercises always suggests students to consult Baidu, Google, or electronic dictionaries when meeting unfamiliar words, expressions or cultural knowledge, for they are extracurricular "teachers". Teachers should encourage students to study by themselves and help them develop good study habits.

Restricted by vocabulary and grammar in the primary stage, all the conversational texts are situation conversations. In order to make up for the deficiency of primary oral conversations, we add a "how to express" part at the end of the exercises in each lesson. They are actually communicative conversations. Generally speaking, communicative sentences and conversations are less situational. It should be noted that this part is prepared for students to study on their own instead of being taught in class.

The well-known sayings in the exercises are for students to study on their own. The purpose is to guide students to perceive the rhymes in the poems so as to develop their interests in reading aloud and lay a foundation for their further study. It is useful for students to get an initial understanding of some poems and sentences we are familiar with.

We sincerely appreciate the guidance and help from friend in this field, as well as the strong support by Beijing Language and Culture University Press when compiling this coursebook.

Compilers

In June 2019

致学习者

亲爱的同学们：

当你拿起这本书，开始学习汉语口语的时候，你的人生便开始了新的旅程。

当你离开家乡，告别父母、兄弟、同学、朋友来到中国这个陌生的国度的时候，你可能有诸多的不适应。

不过没关系。任何人初到异国他乡，都会有这种感觉的。

初来乍到，一句汉语也不会说，一个汉字也不认识，一个朋友都没有，你会感到孤单、寂寞，你会感到无助、痛苦。想家，想爸爸妈妈，想兄弟姐妹，想同学朋友，甚至会哭鼻子，恨不得马上飞回国去。

不过，你一定明白，眼前的这些困难都是暂时的，很快就会过去；过去了，你将由此踏上成才之路。

你要想到自己的未来，想到你是在学习人类最美的语言之一，也是当今世界历史最悠久、使用人数最多的语言之一——汉语！

汉语之美，美不胜收；汉字之妙，妙不可言。

要让自己冷静下来，想一想：今后的路该怎么走？

不必讳言，对于来自世界各国的学习者来说，汉语的确很难学。尽管书里说不难，但是老师心里明白，学好一种外语，对谁来说都不容易。

但“艰难困苦，玉汝于成”，“吃得苦中苦，才有甜上甜”。不经历风雨，难以见彩虹，没有人能随随便便地成功。希望你放平心态，放松心情，准备迎接各种挑战。为了你，为了你的家人，相信你一定不怕苦、不怕难，勇敢地闯过一道道难关，胜利到达成功的彼岸，实现自己美好的理想，成就自己理想的人生。

为此，根据我们几十年教外国留学生的经验，向同学们提出以下几点希望。

1. 无论如何，都应该坚持每天到教室上课

学得好的学生不一定是班上最聪明的学生，但一定是最努力的学生。希望同学们能天天和你的老师、同学见面，天天和他们一起度过这愉快美好的课堂时光。上课不仅仅是学汉语，更是为了培养自己高尚的人品和高贵的人格，使自己成为一个自律且优秀的人。

2. 课后一定要认真做练习

学习外语，遇到不会、不懂的词语和句子是难免的。如今是网络时代，只要你想学，处处都能找到老师。所以我们一再强调：问百度、问谷歌、查电子词典。

要努力培养自己的自学能力。可以说，没有自学能力的人不可能成才。世界上凡是学有所成的人，都有非凡的自学能力。

老师领进门，修行在个人。

那些杰出的、优秀的人虽然都有老师，但他们最后都比自己的老师更优秀！也希望你们能踏着老师的肩膀，奋勇地攀登你们人生的高峰。

3. 要预习，预习比复习更重要

要变“要我学”为“我要学”，使自己时时处于主动的地位。

我们说预习比复习更重要，就是因为预习是你在主动地学。

学习外语，一定要走在老师的前边。现在的学习条件这么好，只要你有志气、肯努力，就要在上课前，把第二天要学的课文、生词都预习预习，一遍、两遍……，或者读一读、记一记。这样，你到教室去上课，将不会再有“难”的苦恼，而会觉得是一种美妙的享受。

4. 多和中国人交往

语言是交际的工具。到生活中去，到中国社会中去，社会生活永远有课堂上学不到的东西。要相信，人类的大多数都是善良的，中国人也一样。只要你不怕、不害羞，你就会明白，在家靠父母，出门靠朋友。多交朋友，一定是一件非常惬意的事。在中国人面前说汉语，不要怕说错。要多说，一次说错了，再说一次可能就说对了。要不了多久，你一定能说一口流利的汉语，你的生活也会开辟一片新的天地。

至于将来做什么，将来会怎么样，请你多读书，书会告诉你的。

这本书和教这本书的老师都是你的朋友，他们将陪伴你一路走去，走向你理想的未来。

最想说的是：我们爱你们，所以献上这本书！

编者

2019 年 6 月初稿

2021 年 2 月定稿

Words for learners

Dear students:

When you pick up this book and begin to learn spoken Chinese, your will start a new journey in your life.

When you leave your hometown, say goodbye to your parents, siblings, classmates and friends, and come to China—an unfamiliar country, you may feel much unadapted.

But it doesn't matter. Any new arrival to an alien place will have the same feeling.

When you first arrive in China, you cannot speak a word of Chinese, nor can you recognize any Chinese characters, or have any friends. You feel lonely, helpless and miserable. You miss your parents, siblings, classmates and friends. You even want to cry. You wish you would fly home immediately.

However, you must know that these immediate difficulties are temporary and will soon be overcome. When you overcome them, you will be on the road to success.

You have to think about your future, and that you are studying one of the most beautiful human languages, as well as one of the oldest and most spoken languages in the world today—Chinese!

The beauty of Chinese is too much to absorb. The wonder of Chinese characters is beyond expression.

You should calm yourself down and think about your road in future.

There is no denying the fact that Chinese is really difficult for students from all over the world. Although it is said in the books that Chinese is not difficult, teachers know that studying a foreign language well is not easy for anyone.

However, no pains, no gains. We hope that you will be prepared for challenges in a peaceful state of mind. For you and your family, we believe you won't be afraid of the difficulties and hardships, and you will get over the hurdles bravely before reaching the dreamland of success, realizing your goals, and achieving your ideal life.

To this end, based on our decades of experience in teaching foreign students, we hope you can do as follows:

1. Persist in attending class every day in any case

Those who do well in class are not necessarily the smartest students, but surely the most hard-working ones. We hope you can meet your teacher and classmates every day and spend the happy time with them in class. By attending class, you not only learn Chinese, but also cultivate noble character and make yourself a self-disciplined and excellent person.

2. Do exercises carefully after class

When studying a foreign language, it is inevitable to encounter words and sentences that you don't know or understand. In this Internet age, teachers can be found everywhere if you want to learn something. That's why we emphasize again and again that you should consult Baidu, Google, and electronic dictionaries.

Efforts should be made to develop your self-study ability. A person without the self study ability cannot be successful. Anyone in the world who is successful in learning has an extraordinary self-study ability.

The teacher may teach, but progress is up to the hard work of the individual.

Those outstanding people have teachers, but they become more excellent than their teachers in the end! We also hope that you can also stand on the shoulders of your teachers and climb the peak of your life bravely.

3. Pay attention to previewing, which is more important than reviewing

Change "make me study" to "I want to study", and take the initiative all the time. Previewing is more important than reviewing in that you are studying on your own initiative when you preview.

When you learn a foreign language, be sure to stay ahead of your teachers. Now the learning conditions are good. As long as you are ambitious and hardworking, you can preview, read and memorize the text and new words several times before class. In this way, when you go to class, you will feel wonderful rather than difficult.

4. Make more contact with Chinese people

Language is a tool of communication. You should experience Chinese life and society, where you can learn what you cannot learn in class. People are mostly kind, so are Chinese. As long as you are not afraid or shy, you will find that you need the support of friends when away from home. It is very pleasant to make more friends. Don't be afraid of making mistakes when speaking Chinese in front of Chinese people. Talk more. If you make a mistake at first, try again and you will probably be right. You will shortly be able to speak Chinese fluently. In addition, you will explore a new world in your life.

As to your future, read more books and you will find the answer.

Both this coursebook and the teacher who uses it in class are your friends, who will accompany you all the way to your ideal future.

What we want to say most is that we offer this book because we love you!

Compilers

First draft in June 2019

Final version in February 2021

一、汉语词类简称表

名称	简称	英文
1. 名词 míngcí	名	noun
2. 代词 dàicí	代	pronoun
3. 动词 dòngcí	动	verb
4. 助动词 zhùdòngcí	助动	auxiliary verb
5. 形容词 xíngróngcí	形	adjective
6. 数词 shùcí	数	numeral
7. 量词 liàngcí	量	measure word
8. 副词 fùcí	副	adverb
9. 介词 jiècí	介	preposition
10. 连词 liáncí	连	conjunction
11. 叹词 tàncí	叹	interjection
12. 拟声词 nǐshēngcí	拟声	onomatopoeia
13. 助词 zhùcí	助	particle
14. 词头 cítóu	头	prefix
15. 词尾 cíwěi	尾	suffix

二、汉语语法术语

1. 主语 zhǔyǔ　subject
2. 谓语 wèiyǔ　predicate
3. 宾语 bīnyǔ　object
4. 定语 dìngyǔ　attribute
5. 状语 zhuàngyǔ　adverbial
6. 补语 bǔyǔ　complement

（1）程度补语 chéngdù bǔyǔ　Degree complement

例如：形容词 + 极了

这个电影好极了。

（2）状态补语 zhuàngtài bǔyǔ　　State complement

例如：动词＋得＋形容词 / 动词短语

他学得好不好？他学得很好。

他跑得快不快？他跑得不快。

你写得怎么样？我写得不太好。

他高兴得跳了起来。

（3）结果补语 jiéguǒ bǔyǔ　　Result complement

例如：动词＋动词 / 形容词

我的作业做完了。

瓶子里的酒喝光了。

他把这本书翻译成了英语。

（4）趋向补语 qūxiàng bǔyǔ　　Complement of direction

例如：动词＋来 / 去 / 上 / 下 / 进 / 出 / 回 / 过 / 起 / 上来 / 下去 / 回来 / 回去 / 过来 / 过去 / 起来 / 进来 / 进去……

他从楼上下来了。

我们从这儿上去吧。

我买回来一盆花。

他从外边里带进来一只小狗。

（5）可能补语 kěnéng bǔyǔ　　Complement of potentiality

例如：动词＋得 / 不＋结果补语 / 趋向补语

中文报你看得懂看不懂？

我现在还听不懂中文广播。

屋子太小，坐不下二十个人。

你买得太多了，我吃不了。

沙发太大，搬不进去。

太重了，我提不动。

（6）数量补语 shùliàng bǔyǔ　　Complement of quantity

例如：动词＋数量短语

他比我高五厘米。

姐姐比我大两岁。

（7）时量补语 shíliàng bǔyǔ　　Complement of duration

例如：动词 + 时量短语

我已经学了<u>一年</u>了。

他来了快<u>一个月</u>了。

（8）动量补语 dòngliàng bǔyǔ　　Complement of frequency

例如：动词 + 动量短语

我敲了<u>一下</u>门，但是没有人答应。

中国我已经来过<u>两次</u>了。

我把这篇文章从头到尾仔细看了<u>一遍</u>，没有发现错字。

香港我去过<u>一回</u>，台湾我还没有去过。

目录 Contents

Dì-sānshísān kè　Wǒ xiǎng dāng yì míng zhìyuànzhě

第三十三课　我想当一名志愿者

Lesson 33　I want to be a volunteer

一　课文 Text

（一）你以前是不是来过中国

（玛丽和山本在聊天儿）

玛丽：山本，我看你对中国的情况挺了解的，你以前是不是来过中国啊？

山本：来过啊，我上大学时来旅行过两次呢。

玛丽：都去过哪些地方？

山本：去过好多地方呢。北边到过哈尔滨，南边去过昆明、桂林、杭州、上海、苏州，西边去过西安和敦煌，东边爬过泰山，还参观过孔子的故乡。

玛丽：你去过的地方可真不少，去过西藏没有？

山本：还没有，不过我很想去。

玛丽：我也特想去那儿看看。

山本：那寒假咱们一起去吧。

玛丽：好啊！

（二）我想当一名志愿者

玛丽：我再问你一个问题，好吗？

山本：你真的想当记者呀？现在就练习采访了。你问吧，只要我知道的就一定回答你。

玛丽：我想问问你，你的理想是什么？

山本：我没有什么远大的理想。我就是想回国以后，在成家立业以前，先去养老院当两年志愿者，照顾那些孤寡老人，让他们能够安度晚年。

玛丽：我觉得你的理想不但远大，而且伟大啊！

山本：哪里。你知道，日本是个老龄化社会，养老是个很大的问题，为了我们老的时候有人照顾，我们现在就应该付出。

玛丽：怪不得你一到周末就到养老院去当志愿者，原来你有这样一个美好的理想。

山本：我去那里实习，为那些爷爷奶奶服务，跟他们聊天儿，也是在练习说汉语呀！

玛丽：你去的那个养老院在什么 地方？

山本：就在西山。

玛丽：我可以跟你去看看吗？

山本：你想去采访吗？

玛丽：不是啊，我也想当几天志愿者。

二 生词 New Words

1	志愿者	zhìyuànzhě	名	volunteer
2	情况	qíngkuàng	名	situation; condition
3	以前	yǐqián	名	before
4	参观	cānguān	动	visit
5	故乡	gùxiāng	名	hometown

6 寒假	hánjià	名	winter vacation; winter holiday
7 采访	cǎifǎng	动	interview
8 远大	yuǎndà	形	lofty
9 成家立业	chéngjiā-lìyè		get married and start one's career
10 养老院	yǎnglǎoyuàn	名	nursing home; old people's home
养老	yǎng lǎo	动	(provide) elderly care
11 照顾	zhàogù	动	take care of; look after
12 孤寡	gūguǎ	形	widowed
13 安度	āndù	动	spend one's remaining years in comfort
14 晚年	wǎnnián	名	old age; senectitude; one's later years
15 伟大	wěidà	形	great
16 老龄化	lǎolínghuà		ageing (process); ageing trend
化	huà	后缀	-ize; -ity
17 付出	fùchū	动	pay; expend
18 怪不得	guàibude	副	no wonder
19 原来	yuánlái	副、形	originally; as a matter of fact; original
20 美好	měihǎo	形	fine; glorious
21 实习	shíxí	动	practice; do an internship

专名 Zhuānmíng Proper Nouns

1 哈尔滨	Hā'ěrbīn	Harbin
2 昆明	Kūnmíng	Kunming
3 桂林	Guìlín	Guilin
4 杭州	Hángzhōu	Hangzhou

5	上海	Shànghǎi	Shanghai
6	苏州	Sūzhōu	Suzhou
7	西安	Xī'ān	Xi'an
8	敦煌	Dūnhuáng	Dunhuang
9	泰山	Tài Shān	Mount Tai
10	孔子	Kǒngzǐ	Confucius
11	西藏	Xīzàng	Tibet
12	西山	Xī Shān	a mountain in Beijing

三 注释 Notes

(一) 动词 + 过

动词后边带动态助词“过”表示动作发生在过去。该动作不延续到现在，强调过去的某种经历。例如：

If a verb is followed by the aspect particle “过”, it indicates that the action happened in the past and has stopped. “Verb + 过” emphasizes a past experience. For example:

1. 你以前是不是来过中国？
2. 我已经去过长城了。
3. 这个电影我看过。

否定式：没（有）+ 动词 + 过 The negative form: 没（有）+ verb + 过

例如：For example:

1. 我从来没有做过按摩（ànmó, massage）。
2. 我还没吃过北京烤鸭。

(二) 怪不得……原来……

“怪不得”表示“明白了原因，不觉得奇怪”，多用于句首，也可以用于第二个小句。原因在文中有交代，常与“原来”呼应。例如：

"怪不得" indicates "having understood the reason and not feeling strange". It is often used at the beginning of a sentence or the second clause. The reason is given in the article, which often echos "原来". For example:

1. 怪不得好几天没见他来上课，原来是病了。
2. 怪不得你买这么漂亮的花，原来是给玛丽过生日呀。

（三）就是

副词"就是"表示确定范围、排除其他，有"只是"的意思。交际中有时带有不如意、不满意、挑剔的意味。例如：

The adverb "就是" means "to determine the scope and exclude others", with the meaning of "just". It sometimes indicates unhappiness, unsatisfaction and pickiness in communication. For example:

1. 我就是想当一名志愿者。
2. 别人都同意，就是你不同意。（也可以说：就你不同意）
3. 大家吃了都没事，就是我一个人吃了拉肚子。（也可以说：就我一个人吃了拉肚子）
4. 这个学生很聪明，就是不努力。

四 练习 Exercises

（一）朗读下列发音相近的词语 Read aloud the following words with similar pronunciation

liǎojiě 了解	liǎojié 了结	yǐqián 以前	yìqiān 一千
gùxiāng 故乡	gǔ xiàng 古巷	hánjià 寒假	hángjia 行家
jìzhě 记者	jízhe 急着	huídá 回答	wěidà 伟大

（二）替换并朗读 Replace and read aloud

1. 我看你对中国的情况挺了解的。

足球	了解
这份工作	喜欢
她	佩服
这事儿	关心
他	放心
这道题	清楚

2. 你是不是来过中国啊？

爬	长城
参观	养老院
问	他
去	西藏
采访	山本
读	这本书

3. 我上大学时来中国旅行过两次。

去西藏	玩儿	一次
腿	受伤	一次
去泰山	爬	两次
到南极 (nánjí, the Antarctic)	旅行	一次
来中国	留学	一年

4. 我没有什么远大的理想，
就是想回国后，当一名志愿者。

汉语老师　记者　工人
编辑（biānji, editor）　警察

（三）**选词填空并朗读下列句子** Choose the appropriate words to fill in the blanks and read aloud the following sentences

几　跟　不过　就　当　挺　不但　好

1. A：我看你对中国的情况________了解的，你以前是不是来过中国？
   B：来过啊，我上大学时来旅行过两次呢。
2. A：你都去过哪些地方？
   B：去过________多地方呢。北边到过哈尔滨，南边去过昆明、桂林、杭州、上海、苏州，西边去过西安和敦煌，东边爬过泰山，还参观过孔子的故乡。
3. A：你去过的地方可真不少，去过西藏没有？
   B：还没有，________我很想去。
4. A：我想问问你，你的理想是什么？
   B：我没有什么远大的理想。我就是想回国后，在成家立业以前，先去养老院________两年志愿者。
5. A：我觉得你的理想________远大，而且伟大啊！
   B：哪里。你知道，日本是个老龄化社会，养老是个很大的问题，为了我们老的时候有人照顾，我们现在就应该付出。
6. 怪不得你一到周末________到养老院去当志愿者，原来你有这样一个美好的理想。
7. 我去那里实习，为那些爷爷奶奶服务，________他们聊天儿，也是在练习说汉语呀！
8. A：你想去采访吗？
   B：不是啊，我也想当________天志愿者。

（四）**将 A、B 两列连线，组成正确的复句** Match A with B to make correct complex sentences

1.

A	B
他不但聪明，	而且我妹妹也来了。
他不但英语好，	而且也喜欢打太极拳。
这个超市的东西不但好，	而且汉语也说得很流利（liúlì, fluently）。
她不但人长得漂亮，	而且非常努力。
她不但喜欢爬山，	而且也很便宜。
不但我来中国学习汉语，	而且温柔（wēnróu, gentle and soft）善良（shànliáng, kind-hearted）。

2.

A	B
怪不得你买这么漂亮的花，	原来课文她都能背下来了。
怪不得她那么高兴，	原来护照找不着了。
怪不得接不到你的电话，	原来是给朋友过生日呀。
怪不得她汉语说得那么流利，	因为上课，她把手机关了。
怪不得她那么着急，	她都学了四年了。
怪不得她回答得那么好，	原来她妈妈要来中国了。

（五）**回答课文的问题** Answer the questions about the text

1. 山本来过中国没有？她来过几次？
2. 山本都去过什么地方？
3. 山本还想去什么地方旅行？
4. 玛丽想不想去西藏？
5. 玛丽想当什么？
6. 山本回国后想做什么工作？

（六）**你是 A，请你向 B 提问** Supposing you are A, ask B questions

1. A：________________________________？

   B：我以前没有来过中国，这是第一次。

2. A：________________________________？

B：来以前我对中国的情况很不了解。

3. A：________________________________？

B：我在我们国家学过一点儿汉语。

4. A：________________________________？

B：因为学习的时间很短，又常常不上课，所以我汉语说得不好。

5. A：________________________________？

B：我爸爸希望我学好汉语，因为他的公司与中国一家公司有业务来往（láiwǎng, business dealings）。

6. A：________________________________？

B：将来做什么，我还没想好。

（七）**根据实际情况回答问题** Answer the questions according to your actual situations

1. 你都去过哪些国家？
2. 你以前来过中国没有？
3. 你来过几次中国？去过哪些地方？
4. 你认识几个中国人？
5. 你吃过哪些中国美食？
6. 你想不想到西藏和新疆去看看？

（八）**和同学一起表演课文** Act out the text with your classmates

（九）**读后说** Read the passage and say it

昨天晚上我和山本聊天儿，聊得很愉快。我觉得山本对中国的情况很了解，就问她以前是不是来过中国。她说她上大学时来旅行过两次，去过好多地方。

我问山本的理想是什么，她说自己没有什么远大的理想，就是想回国后去养老院当一名志愿者，照顾那些孤寡老人，让他们安度晚年。怪不得她来中国后，经常去一家养老院实习。她说，为老人们服务、跟老人聊天儿很愉快，同时也练习了汉语。我也想跟她去当几天志愿者。

（十）怎么表达 How to express

zháo mí
着 迷　obsession

Wǒ míshang tā le.
1. 我 迷上 它了。
I'm hooked on it.

Wǒ duì wǎngshàng de yóuxì zháo mí.
2. 我 对 网上 的游戏 着 迷。
I'm crazy about online games.

Wǒ shì gè zúqiúmí.
3. 我 是 个足球迷。
I'm a soccer fan.

（十一）朗读中国经典诗词，请注意语音语调 Read aloud the classic Chinese poem and pay attention to the pronunciation and intonation

Mò Méi
墨 梅

[Yuán] Wáng Miǎn
[元] 王 冕（1287—1359）

Wǒ jiā xǐyànchí tóu shù, duǒduǒ huā kāi dàn mò hén.
我家洗砚池头树，朵朵 花开淡 墨 痕。
Búyào rén kuā hǎo yánsè, zhǐ liú qīngqì mǎn qiánkūn.
不要人 夸 好 颜色，只留清气 满 乾坤。

（十二）请欣赏下列著名的词句 Please enjoy the following famous saying

Àirénzhě, rén héng ài zhī.
爱人者，人 恒 爱之。

He who loves others is always loved by others.

Dì-sānshísì kè Nǐ jiànguo dàxióngmāo méiyǒu

第三十四课 你见过大熊猫没有

Lesson 34 Have you ever seen a giant panda?

一 课文 Text

A：你见过大熊猫没有？

B：见过了，上个星期天去动物园看的。你见过吗？

A：我只在电视上看见过，还没亲眼见过呢。

B：大熊猫什么时候看都觉得好玩儿。

A：是，它那憨态可掬的样子很可爱。

B：那天我去看的时候，它懒洋洋地躺在树上，游客怎么逗它，它也不下来。一看见饲养员端来了好吃的，就连滚带爬地下来了，还抱住饲养员的腿，不让她走，可好玩儿了。

A：我小侄子发来微信，要我拍一些大熊猫的照片和视频给他发过去，所以，我得去一趟动物园。

B：不过，周六周日去，看大熊猫的人太多了。

A：那没办法，大熊猫无论什么时候、无论在哪儿都很受欢迎呀！不管怎样，我得满足孩子的心愿。

二 生词 New Words

1	动物园	dòngwùyuán	名	zoo
2	亲眼	qīnyǎn	副	with one's own eyes
3	憨态可掬	hāntài-kějū		charmingly naive
4	样子	yàngzi	名	look; appearance
5	可爱	kě'ài	形	lovely; cute
6	懒洋洋	lǎnyángyáng	形	lazy; languid; listless
7	躺	tǎng	动	lie
8	游客	yóukè	名	visitor; tourist
9	逗	dòu	动	tantalize
10	看见	kàn jiàn	动	see
11	饲养员	sìyǎngyuán	名	feeder; breeder
12	端	duān	动	hold sth. level with both hands; carry
13	连滚带爬	liángǔn-dàipá		roll and crawl
	连…带…	lián…dài…		*indicating two actions almost taking place at the same time*
14	抱	bào	动	hold or carry in the arms
15	住	zhù	动	*used after a verb as a complement*
16	侄子	zhízi	名	nephew
17	得	děi	动	must
18	趟	tàng	量	*a measure word for trips to and fro*
19	办法	bànfǎ	名	way; method
20	无论	wúlùn	连	whatever; regardless of
21	受	shòu	动	receive
22	欢迎	huānyíng	动	welcome

23 满足	mǎnzú	动	satisfy
24 孩子	háizi	名	child
25 心愿	xīnyuàn	名	wish

三 注释 Notes

(一) 任指（泛指）

“什么”“怎么”等疑问代词可以用来表示任指，常用在“都”或“也”的前面。例如：

Some interrogative pronouns, such as “什么” and “怎么”, can be used to indicate arbitrary reference. They are often used before “都” or “也”. For example:

1. 大熊猫什么时候看都觉得好玩儿。

句子中的“什么”表示任指（泛指），“什么时候”的意思是：任何时候。

“什么” in the sentence means “any”, “什么时候” means “any time”.

2. 游客怎么逗它，它也不下来。

句子中的“怎么”表示任指（泛指），“怎么逗它”的意思是：这么逗它，那么逗它，它都……

“怎么” in the sentence means “whatever”, and “怎么逗它” “means no matter how you tantalize it, it will...”

(二) 连…带…

“连…带…”连接两个动词，表示两个动作几乎同时发生。例如：

“连……带……” is used to connect two verbs to show two actions almost happening at the same time. For example:

1. 她连说带笑，看样子非常高兴。
2. 孩子连蹦带跳地跑了过来。
3. 这顿饭，我们连做带吃，一共用了两个小时。

（三）比较："过"与"了"

"过"和"了"都可以用在动词后，表示动作的完成。

"过" and "了" are used after verbs to indicate the completion of actions.

1. 否定式不同 Their negative forms differ.

过：没（有）+ 动词 + 过

了：没（有）+ 动词（不能有"了"）

例如：For example:

（1）A：你见过大熊猫吗？

B：我见过 / 没见过。

（2）A：昨天晚上的电视你看了吗？

B：我没看。（不能说：* 我没看了）

2. 句子的意思有差别 The meanings of the sentences also differ.

例如：For example:

（1）我学了半年汉语。（现在学不学不确定）

我学过半年汉语。（现在不学了）

（2）他上周去了中国。（现在还在中国）

他上周去过中国。（现在在不在中国不确定）

四 练习 Exercises

（一）朗读下列发音相近的词语 Read aloud the following words with similar pronunciation

diànshì 电视	tiānshǐ 天使	dòngwù 动物	dòng wǔ 动 武
yàngzi 样子	yànzi 燕子	bàozhù 抱住	bàozhú 爆竹
búguò 不过	bǔ guò 补过	zhízi 侄子	zhìcǐ 至此

（二）替换并朗读 Replace and read aloud

1. A：你见过大熊猫没有？
   B：见过 / 没见过。

吃	元宵（yuánxiāo, glutinous rice dumpling）
去 / 来	中国
喝	普洱茶（pǔ'ěrchá, Pu'er tea）
爬	泰山
看	京剧（jīngjù, Beijing opera）
学	太极拳

2. 我觉得熊猫很好玩儿。

小侄子很可爱　这首歌很好听
这个菜很好吃　这种茶很好喝
这个游戏很好玩儿
汉语越学越有意思

3. 那天我去看的时候，它懒洋洋地躺在树上，不下来。

发现看熊猫的人很多
他正在弹琴呢
她懒洋洋地在床上躺着呢
她正在看电视
她正在练健美操呢
他正在拿着手机玩儿游戏

4. 因为小侄子要我拍一些大熊猫的照片和视频给他发过去，所以我得去一次 / 趟动物园。

一个国内的好朋友
一个网站　一家电视台
我的男 / 女朋友
我奶奶 / 爷爷

（三）**选词填空并朗读下列句子** Choose the appropriate words to fill in the blanks and read aloud the following sentences

过 的 就 满足 过去 什么

1. A：你见过大熊猫没有？
   B：见过了，上个星期天去动物园看________。
2. 我只在电视上看见________，还没亲眼见过呢。
3. 大熊猫________时候看都觉得好玩儿。它那憨态可掬的样子很可爱。
4. 那天我去看的时候，它懒洋洋地躺在树上，游客怎么逗它，它也不下来。一看见饲养员端来了好吃的，________连滚带爬地下来了。还抱住饲养员的腿，不让她走，可好玩儿了。
5. 我小侄子发来微信，要我拍一些大熊猫的照片和视频给他发________，所以，我得去一趟动物园。
6. 那没办法，大熊猫无论什么时候、无论在哪儿都很受欢迎呀！不管怎样，我得________孩子的心愿。

（四）**完成下列会话并大声朗读** Complete the following conversations and read them aloud

1. A：________________________________？
   B：我见过大熊猫了，上个星期天去动物园看的。
2. A：________________________________？（做什么）
   B：那天我去看的时候，它懒洋洋地躺在树上，游客怎么逗它，它也不下来。
3. A：大熊猫为什么连滚带爬地从树上下来？
   B：________________________________。
4. A：________________________________？
   B：它那憨态可掬的样子很可爱。
5. A：________________________________？（为什么）
   B：我小侄子发来微信，要我拍一些大熊猫的照片和视频给他发过去。所以，我得去一趟。

6. A：不过，你周六周日去的话，看大熊猫的人太多了。

B：____。（无论　不管）

（五）**你是A，请你向B提问** Supposing you are A, ask B questions

1. A：____？

B：我以前没有来过中国。

2. A：____？

B：我还没去过长城。

3. A：____？

B：我也想去看看大熊猫。

4. A：____？

B：我只学过一点儿汉语。

5. A：____？

B：只学了半年，还不太会说。

6. A：____？

B：来中国以后，我还没有去旅行过。

7. A：____？

B：我很想去长城看看。

（六）**跟同学一起练习下面的会话** Practice the following conversation with your classmates

看京剧

甲：你看过京剧吗？

乙：看过。

甲：你是在哪儿看的。

乙：在一个茶馆儿（cháguǎnr, teahouse）看的。

甲：你觉得怎么样？

乙：我听不懂，但是能明白大概意思。因为老师讲过那个故事（gùshi, story）。

甲：我也看过一次，一句也听不懂。不过，我喜欢京剧的脸谱（liǎnpǔ, facial make-up）。

乙：我也特喜欢，还买了一个挂（guà, hang）在了我宿舍里。

（**提示：**不认识的词，请问百度 / 谷歌。）

(**Reminder:** Search on Baidu/Google for the words you don't know.)

（七）根据实际情况回答问题 Answer the questions according to your actual situations

1. 你现在住的城市的动物园里有大熊猫吗？
2. 你亲眼看过大熊猫没有？
3. 来中国以后你去过什么地方？
4. 你听过中国歌吗？听过什么歌？
5. 你看过中国电影吗？看过什么电影？
6. 你读过翻译（fānyì, translate）的中文书吗？

（八）和同学一起表演课文 Act out the text with your classmates

（九）读后说 Read the passages and say it

1. 上个星期天我去动物园看了大熊猫。大熊猫真是可爱！我去看它的时候，它懒洋洋地躺在一棵树上，游客怎么逗它，它也不下来，好像在睡觉。过了一会儿，饲养员端着吃的来了。它一看见饲养员就连滚带爬地从树上下来了，还高兴地抱住饲养员的腿，不让她走，特好玩儿。

2. 我以前只在电视上看过大熊猫，它憨态可掬的样子，非常可爱。我的小侄子给我发微信，说他想看大熊猫的照片和视频，问我能不能去动物园拍了发给他。所以我想抽空儿去一次动物园，拍些大熊猫的照片和视频，满足孩子的心愿。

(十) 怎么表达 How to express

chēngzàn
称赞 compliments

Duō kě'ài de dàxióngmāo a!
1. 多可爱的 大熊猫 啊!

What a lovely giant panda!

Tā hěn yǒu yōumògǎn.
2. 他 很 有 幽默感。

He has a good sense of humor.

Tā xǐhuan bāngzhù rén. / Tā lèyú-zhùrén.
3. 他 喜欢 帮助 人。/他 乐于助人。

He likes helping others.

(十一) 朗读中国经典诗词，请注意语音语调 Read aloud the classic Chinese poem and pay attention to the pronunciation and intonation

Zǎo Fā Báidì Chéng
早发白帝 城

[Táng] Lǐ Bái
[唐] 李 白 (701—762)

Zhāo cí Báidì cǎiyún jiān, qiān lǐ Jiānglíng yí rì huán.
朝 辞 白帝 彩云 间，千 里 江陵 一日 还。

Liǎng'àn yuán shēng tí bú zhù, qīngzhōu yǐ guò wàn chóng shān.
两 岸 猿 声 啼不住，轻舟 已过 万 重 山。

(十二) 请欣赏下列著名的词句 Please enjoy the following famous saying

Bǎi wén bùrú yí jiàn.
百 闻 不如 一 见。

Seeing is believing.

Dì-sānshíwǔ kè 第三十五课 Lesson 35

Zhè shuāng bǐ nà shuāng hǎokàn 这双比那双好看 This pair looks better than that one

一 课文 Text

（在鞋店）

A：欢迎光临！

B：我想看看皮鞋。

A：你穿多大号的？

B：三十六号的。

A：你看这几双怎么样？

B：这双跟那双的质量一样吗？

A：质量一样，都是牛皮的，就是颜色不一样。

B：我觉得这双黑的比那双咖啡色的好看。

A：这双比那双贵一百多块钱呢。你喜不喜欢这种样式的？

B：这双样子没有那双好看。

A：你再看看这双。这双比那几双的质量都好。

B：看起来不错，我试试可以吗？

A：当然可以。

B：我试了试。这双有点儿小，有没有大一点儿的？

A：给你换一双，你再试试这双。

B：这双不大不小正合适，穿着很舒服。这双多少钱？

A：四百八。

B：四百八？贵了点儿，能不能便宜点儿？

A：你真想要的话，给四百五吧。

B：四百行不行？

A：四百不行。一分价钱一分货，这是名牌儿。

B：那给我拿一双吧。

二 生词 New Words

1	双	shuāng	量	pair
2	比	bǐ	介、动	than
3	光临	guānglín	动	presence (of a guest, etc.)
4	皮鞋	píxié	名	leather shoes
5	质量	zhìliàng	名	quality
6	牛皮	niúpí	名	cattle hide
7	颜色	yánsè	名	color
8	样式	yàngshì	名	style; design
9	看起来	kàn qǐlái		it looks
	起来	qǐlái	动	*used after a verb to indicate estimation or express an opinion*
10	换	huàn	动	exchange
11	合适	héshì	形	suitable
12	……的话	…dehuà	助	(*used at the end of a conditional clause*) if
13	一分价钱一分货	yì fēn jiàqián yì fēn huò		you get what you pay for
	分	fēn	量	*a measure word*

价钱	jiàqián	名	price
货	huò	名	goods
14 名牌儿	míngpáir	名	famous brand

三 注释 Notes

(一) 比较句：跟……一样 / 不一样

"A 跟 B 一样"表示比较的结果相同。例如：

"A 跟 B 一样" is used to indicate the comparison results are the same. For example:

A	B	
这双黑皮鞋 400 元。	那双咖啡色的 400 元。	→ 这双皮鞋跟那双价钱一样。
小王 20 岁。	小张也 20 岁。	→ 小王跟小张一样大。
我喜欢听音乐。	她也喜欢听音乐。	→ 她跟我一样喜欢听音乐。

"A 跟 B 不一样"表示比较的结果不同。例如：

"A 跟 B 不一样" indicates the comparison results are not the same. For example:

A	B	
这本书 20 元。	那本书 40 元。	→ 这本书跟那本书价钱不一样。
这双鞋是牛皮的。	那双鞋是布的。	→ 这双鞋跟那双的材质（cáizhì, material）不一样。

(二)"比"字句

比较两个事物之间的差别时用"比"字句。

"比" sentence is used to show the difference between two things.

1. A 比 B + 形容词　A 比 B + adjective

例如：For example:

（1）飞机比汽车快。

（2）西瓜比苹果大。

（3）大象比大熊猫重。

否定式：B+ 没有 + A + 形容词

The negative form: B + 没有 + A + adjective

例如：For example:

（1）飞机比火车快。→ 火车没有飞机快。

（2）西瓜比苹果大。→ 苹果没有西瓜大。

（3）大象比大熊猫重。→ 大熊猫没有大象重。

在“比”字句里，如果谓语是形容词，形容词前不能用“很、真、非常”等副词。例如：

In a “ 比 ” sentence, if the predicate is an adjective, it cannot be preceded by such adverbs as “ 很 ” “ 真 ” “ 非常 ”, etc. For example:

不能说：* 西瓜比苹果很大。

* 飞机比汽车很快。

2. A 比 B + 动词 + 宾语　A 比 B + verb + object

例如：For example:

（1）她比我爱爬山。

（2）我比她爱画画儿。

3. A 比 B + 动词 + 得 + 补语 / A + 动词 + 得 + 比 + B + 补语

A 比 B + verb + 得 + complement / A + verb + 得 + 比 + B + complement

如果动词带状态补语，“比……”可以放在动词前，也可以放在补语前。例如：

If a verb is followed by a state complement, “ 比……” can be placed either before the verb or before the complement. For example:

（1）他比我起得早。/ 他起得比我早。

（2）我比他跑得快。/ 我跑得比他快。

（三）有（一）点儿

“有（一）点儿”作状语，用在形容词前，多用于表达不如意的事情。例如：

"有（一）点儿" is used as an adverbial before an adjective, usually expressing something undesirable. For example:

1. 这双有（一）点儿大，有没有小一点儿的？
2. 这双鞋有（一）点儿不合适。[不能说：* 这双鞋有（一）点儿合适。]

四 练习 Exercises

（一）朗读 Read aloud

1. 朗读下列发音相近的词语 Read aloud the following words with similar pronunciation

píxié 皮鞋	píxuē 皮靴	yánsè 颜色	yǎnsè 眼色
guānglín 光临	guāngyīn 光阴	shìshi 试试	shìshí 事实
héshì 合适	hé shí 何时	shūfu 舒服	shūshu 叔叔

2. 朗读下列词组 Read the following phrases aloud

有点儿大	有点儿小	有点儿长	有点儿短
有点儿肥	有点儿瘦	有点儿难	有点儿远
有点儿少	有点儿多	有点儿累	有点儿饿
有点儿困	有点儿渴	有点儿忙	有点儿贵
不大不小	不多不少	不肥不瘦	不长不短
不上不下	不深不浅	不高不低	不近不远

3. 朗读下列句子 Read the following sentences aloud

（1）这个手机跟你的牌子一样。
（2）这辆车跟那辆价钱一样。
（3）你们俩的个子一样高。
（4）她跟她姐姐一样漂亮。

（5）她汉语说得跟中国人一样流利。

（6）你跟爱德华跑得一样快。

（二）**替换并朗读** Replace and read aloud

1. 我想看看<u>皮鞋</u>。

球鞋	拖鞋	大衣
羽绒服	牛仔裤	帽子
夹克	围巾	

2. A：你看看这<u>双</u>怎么样？

   B：这<u>双</u>有点儿<u>小</u>，有没有<u>大</u>一点儿的？

件	肥	瘦
条	长	短
个	薄	厚
个	贵	便宜

（三）**选词填空并朗读下列句子** Choose the appropriate words to fill in the blanks and read aloud the following sentences

双　给　多　的话　着　有点儿

1. A：我想看看皮鞋。

   B：你穿________大号的？

2. A：你看这________怎么样？

   B：这双样子不太好看。

3. A：你再看看这双。

   B：我试了试。这双________小，有没有大一点儿的？

4. 这双不大不小正合适，穿________也很舒服。这双多少钱？

5. A：能不能便宜点儿？

   B：你真想要________，给四百五吧。

6. 那________我拿一双吧。

（四）你是 A，请你向 B 提问 Supposing you are A, ask B questions

1. A：________________________？（词典　用用）
   B：当然可以，你用吧。
2. A：________________________？（大衣　试试）
   B：行，你试吧。
3. A：________________________？
   [这本　杂志（zázhì, magazine）　看看]
   B：你看吧。
4. A：________________________？
   [葡萄（pútao, grape）　尝尝]
   B：当然可以，你尝吧。
5. A：________________________？
   （这条　裙子　穿穿）
   B：你穿穿试试吧。
6. A：________________________？
   （这顶　帽子　戴戴）
   B：可以，你戴戴看吧。

（五）完成下列句子并大声朗读 Complete the following sentences and read them aloud

例：A：这双鞋合适吗？
　　B：我试了试，不大不小，很合适。

1. A：__________合适吗？
   B：我穿了穿，不肥不瘦，正好。
2. A：__________好听吗？
   B：我听了听，很好听。
3. A：__________好看吗？
   B：我看了看，很好看。
4. A：__________好用不好用？
   B：我试了试，很好用。

5. A：__________好玩儿不好玩儿？

B：我玩儿了玩儿，特好玩儿。

（六）将 A、B 两列连线，组成正确的句子，然后朗读 Match A with B to make correct sentences and read them aloud

A	B
飞机	比我好得多。
姐姐	比火车快。
这座楼	比冬天的长。
我没有他	比我大两岁。
她汉语说得	跑得快。
夏天的白天	比那座楼高。

（七）用“比”字句说下列句子 Change the following sentences into “比” sentences

例如：我没有玛丽大。→ 玛丽比我大。

1. 这种颜色没有那种好看。→

____。

2. 我学习没有他那么努力，所以成绩没有他好。→

____。

3. 这座楼没有那座高。→

____。

4. 麦克没有爱德华跑得快。→

____。

5. 这儿的冬天没有我们那儿冷。→

____。

6. 葡萄没有苹果便宜。→

____。

（八）和同学练习说“比较句” Practice comparative sentences with your classmates

例如：

1. A：小张比小李高吗？
   B：小张比小李高。
2. A：小王比小李高吗？
   B：小王没有小李高。

小张	小李	小王	
180 CM	175 CM	170 CM	高
20 岁	19 岁	19 岁	大
95 分	95 分	90 分	学习好
18 秒	17 秒	16 秒	快

（九）和同学一起表演课文 Act out the text with your classmates

（十）读后说 Read the passage and say it

我早就想买一双皮鞋。今天去了一家鞋店，我看那里的皮鞋不错，就试了一双。皮鞋不大不小，挺合适，穿着很舒服。我问店主那双鞋多少钱，她说四百八十元。我觉得贵了点儿，就对她说，能不能便宜点儿，四百可以不可以。她说不行，要是我想要，四百五可以。因为很喜欢这双鞋，所以我就买了。

（十一）怎么表达 How to express

bǐjiào
比较　comparison

Wǒ de Hànyǔ yìtiān bǐ yìtiān hǎo.
1. 我的汉语一天比一天好。
   My Chinese is getting better every day.

Tā de Hànyǔ bǐ guòqù liúlì duō le.
2. 他的 汉语比 过去 流利 多 了。

He speaks Chinese much more fluently than he used to.

Qíngkuàng yì tiān bǐ yì tiān hǎo.
3. 情况 一天 比一天 好。

The situation is getting better every day.

（十二）朗读中国经典诗词，请注意语音语调 Read aloud the classic Chinese poem and pay attention to the pronunciation and intonation

Wàng Tiānmén Shān
望 天门 山

[Táng] Lǐ Bái
［唐］李 白（701—762）

Tiānmén zhōng duàn Chǔ Jiāng kāi, bì shuǐ dōng liú zhì cǐ huí.
天门 中 断 楚 江 开，碧水 东 流 至此回。
Liǎng'àn qīng shān xiāngduì chū, gū fān yí piàn rì biān lái.
两岸 青 山 相对 出，孤帆 一 片 日 边 来。

（十三）请欣赏下列著名的词句 Please enjoy the following famous saying

Dú wàn juàn shū, xíng wàn lǐ lù.
读万 卷 书，行 万里路。

Reading ten thousands of books and traveling ten thousands of miles.

Dì-sānshíliù kè Wǒ de shǒujī yǒu wèntí le

第三十六课 我的手机有问题了

Lesson 36 There's something wrong with my cell phone

一 课文 Text

（一）我的手机有问题了

（在修理店）

A：你能看一下我的手机吗？

B：有什么问题？

A：不知道，您给看看吧。开机不一会儿，就自动关机，一充电就发热。

B：可能是电池的问题，得先检查一下电池。（检查以后）啊，电池老化了，要换新的。换新的吧？

A：换吧！

B：（修理完）已经换上了新电池，你再试试看。

A：好了。多少钱？

B：150 元。

A：我扫码支付吧。

B：好。

A：谢谢您！

B：不客气。

（二）不是电路断了，就是蓄电池有问题

A：这辆电动车不能动了。

B：轮胎没扎破吧？

A：没有。

B：不是电路断了，就是蓄电池有问题。

A：你给检查一下吧。

B：你的电池用了多久了？

A：我也不知道。这是一辆旧车，朋友毕业回国时送给我的。

B：是蓄电池的问题，该换电池了。

A：那就换个新的吧。

B：你得上网去买，我这里没有蓄电池。

A：是吗？网上能买到蓄电池吗？

B：我想能买到吧。

A：买来换上就可以了吗？

B：没问题。不过，说实在的，你这辆车也该换了。

（三）我的自行车坏了，麻烦您给修一下

A：我的自行车坏了，麻烦您给修一下。

B：怎么了？

A：车闸不灵了，后胎慢撒气。

B：（检查以后）你看，内胎破了，外胎也都磨平了，都需要换新的。你先放这儿吧。

A：什么时候能修好？

B：下午来取吧。

A：能不能快点儿？我下午要用。

B：那你中午来取吧。

A：谢谢了。

二 生词 New Words

1	开机	kāi jī	动	switch on
2	自动	zìdòng	副、形	automatically; automatic
3	关机	guān jī	动	switch off
4	发热	fā rè	动	get hot
	发	fā	动	get; send out
	热	rè	形	hot
5	电池	diànchí	名	battery
	蓄电池	xùdiànchí	名	accumulator; storage battery
	蓄	xù	动	store up
6	老化	lǎohuà	动	age; become older
7	扫码	sǎo mǎ	动	scan a QR code
8	轮胎	lúntāi	名	tire
	内胎	nèitāi	名	inner tube
	外胎	wàitāi	名	outer tube
	胎	tāi	名	tire
9	扎	zhā	动	prick
10	破	pò	动	(be) broken
11	电路	diànlù	名	circuit
12	断	duàn	动	break
13	久	jiǔ	形	long

14 毕业	bì yè	动	graduate
15 实在	shízài	副、形	really; indeed
16 修	xiū	动	repair; mend
17 车闸	chēzhá	名	brake
18 灵	líng	形	easy to handle
19 撒气	sā qì	动	leak; get a flat tire
撒	sā	动	leak
20 磨	mó	动	grind
21 平	píng	形	flat
22 取	qǔ	动	get; take; fetch

三 注释 Notes

（一）不过

副词“不过”在句中表示转折，语气比“但是”轻。例如：

The adverb “不过” is used to indicate a transition in a sentence, but it is lighter in tone than “不但”. For example:

1. 他汉语说得还可以，不过声调有些问题。
2. 现在我的听说还不错，不过读写困难比较大。

（二）说实在的

“说实在的”是插入语。意思是：告诉对方真实的情况，或提出自己的建议。

“说实在的” is a parenthesis, which means “to tell the other person the truth or offer your own advice”.

四 练习 Exercises

（一）朗读下列发音相近的词语 Read aloud the following words with similar pronunciation

diànchí 电池	tiānchí 天池	xiūlǐ 修理	xiùlì 秀丽
wèntí 问题	wéntǐ 文体	huí guó 回国	huǐguò 悔过
chōng diàn 充电	chóng tián 重填	diànlù 电路	diànlú 电炉

（二）替换并朗读 Replace and read aloud

1. 你再试试看。

穿穿　修修　用用
写写　想想　做做

2. A：怎么了？
   B：电池老化了。

头有点儿疼　手破了
咳嗽得很厉害　发烧了
拉肚子了　感冒了

3. 该换电池了。

手机　车　书
眼镜　鞋　袜子

4. A：买得到买不到蓄电池？
   B：买得到 / 买不到。

买　票
送　学校
开　山顶
学　第三册
看　大熊猫
遇　玛丽

5. 我的<u>自行车</u>坏了，
麻烦您给修一下。

闹钟	手表	眼镜
电脑	拉链儿	

6. 能不能<u>快</u>点儿？

早	便宜	多
大	软	淡

（三）**选词填空并朗读下列句子** Choose the appropriate words to fill in the blanks and read aloud the following sentences

辆　了　该　什么　上　就　检查　破

1. A：你的手机有________问题？
   B：我不知道，开机不一会儿，就自动关机，一充电________发热。
2. 可能是电池的问题，得先________一下电池。啊，是电池老化了，要换新的。
3. 已经换________了新电池，你再试试看。
4. 这辆电动车不能动了。是不是轮胎扎________了？
5. A：不是电路断了，就是蓄电池有问题。你的电池用了多久______？
   B：我也不知道。这是一______旧车，朋友毕业回国时送给我的。
6. 说实在的，你这辆车也________换了。

不　了　好　取　修　用

1. 我的自行车坏了，麻烦您给________一下。
2. 车闸________灵了，后胎慢撒气。
3. 你看，内胎破________，外胎也都磨平了，都需要换新的。你先放这儿吧。

4. A：什么时候能修________？
 B：你下午来取吧。
5. A：能不能快点儿？我下午要________。
 B：那你中午来________吧。

（四）将 A、B 两列连线，组成正确的对话 Match A with B to make correct dialogs

A	B
那个教室坐得下二十个人吗？	我没戴眼镜看不清楚。
你看得见屏幕上的字吗？	对不起，我有事儿，去不了。
这座山你爬得上去吗？	那个教室很大，坐得下。
今天晚上你能去吗？	太高了，我爬不上去。
这些饺子你吃得了吗？	作业不多，我想做得完。
这张桌子你搬得动吗？	没问题，你下午来取吧。
我的车下午修得好吗？	有点儿多，我吃不了。
今天的作业一个小时做得完吗？	太重了，我一个人搬不动。

（五）你是 A，请你向 B 提问 Supposing you are A, ask B questions

1. A：________________________________？（怎么）
 B：我的电动自行车不动了。
2. A：________________________________？（什么）
 B：师傅检查过了，说是电池老化了。
3. A：________________________________？（换）
 B：那个修车的没有蓄电池。
4. A：________________________________？（哪儿）
 B：他说可以到网上去买。
5. A：________________________________？（多久）
 B：这是一辆旧电动车，是朋友回国时送给我的。
6. A：________________________________？（换）
 B：我想换上新电池，再骑半年，我也该回国了。

（六）**根据实际情况回答问题** Answer the questions according to your actual situations

1. 你用的什么手机？
2. 你的手机怎么样？
3. 来中国后，你修过什么东西吗？
4. 你生活中有没有遇到过一些小麻烦？
5. 你每天怎么去上课？（步行 / 坐车 / 骑车）

（七）**和同学一起表演课文** Act out the text with your classmates

（八）**读后说** Read the passage and say it

我的手机有问题了，开不了机了。我想可能是没电了，就马上充电，但充了半天也充不进去，手机还发热。我马上去手机维修店，请他们看看是怎么回事儿。工作人员检查了我的手机，他说是电池老化了，需要换新电池，问我换不换。我回答说当然换。

换上了新电池，手机立即就好了。我很高兴，没有手机的生活真让我受不了啊！

（九）**怎么表达** How to express

gāoxìng 高兴	happiness

Wǒ wèi nǐ gǎndào gāoxìng.
1. 我为你感到高兴。

I'm so happy for you.

Tīngdào zhège xiāoxi, wǒ hěn gāoxìng.
2. 听到这个消息，我很高兴。

I'm very pleased to hear the news.

Tā kǎoshì tōngguòle, hěn gāoxìng.
3. 他考试通过了，很高兴。

He is delighted that he has passed the exam.

（十）朗读中国经典诗词，请注意语音语调 Read aloud the classic Chinese poem and pay attention to the pronunciation and intonation

Féng Xuě Sù Fúróng Shān Zhǔrén
逢 雪 宿 芙蓉 山 主人
[Táng] Liú Chángqīng
［唐］刘 长卿 （？—789）

Rì mù cāngshān yuǎn, tiān hán báiwū pín.
日 暮 苍山 远，天 寒 白屋 贫。
Cháimén wén quǎn fèi, fēngxuě yè guī rén.
柴门 闻 犬 吠，风雪 夜 归 人。

（十一）请欣赏下列著名的词句 Please enjoy the following famous saying

Chē dào shān qián bì yǒu lù.
车 到 山 前 必 有 路。
Things will eventually sort themselves out.

Dì-sānshíqī kè Bié bǎ shénme dōngxi là zài chē shang le

第三十七课 别把什么东西落在车上了

Lesson 37 Don't leave anything in the car

一 课文 Text

（同学三人搭乘出租车去机场）

A：（打电话）喂！是您要的车吧，车已经到您楼下了。

B：好。我们马上下去。

（在楼下）

A：是去机场，对吧？

B：对。把这些行李放到后备箱里去吧。

A：我来放，你们先上车吧。

B：放得下放不下？放不下的话，只把这两个大箱子放进后备箱里，把这个小箱子放到座位上去吧。

A：没问题，都放得下。好了，上车吧。请把车门关上。

B：都上来了，师傅，开车吧。需要多长时间？

A：要看交通情况，不堵车的话，大概 40 多分钟就到了。

B：千万别堵车。

A：每天这个时候都比较堵，不过，我会尽力的。

B：师傅，您不用着急，要注意安全。

A：放心吧，干我们这一行的，什么时候都得把安全放在第一位。安全第一嘛。

（车到机场）

B：到了吧？

A：到了，我把车停在8号门口儿。下车吧，注意别把什么东西落在车上了。祝你们一路平安！

B：知道了，谢谢师傅。

A：不客气。

二 生词 New Words

1	落	là	动	leave behind; forget to bring
2	搭乘	dāchéng	动	travel by (plane, ship, car, etc.)
3	出租车	chūzūchē	名	taxi
4	机场	jīchǎng	名	airport
5	喂	wèi	叹	hello; hey
6	下	xià	动	*indicating the capacity for holding or containing sth.*
7	行李	xíngli	名	luggage
8	后备箱	hòubèixiāng	名	car boot
9	箱子	xiāngzi	名	suitcase
10	放	fàng	动	put; place
11	座位	zuòwèi	名	seat
12	师傅	shīfu	名	*a polite title for one with accomplished skills usually in a trade or handicraft*
13	千万	qiānwàn	副	must; be sure to
14	尽力	jìn lì	动	do all one can; try one's best
15	着急	zháo jí	形	worried

16 行	háng	名	profession; line of business
17 第	dì	前缀	*used to indicate ordinal numbers*
18 位	wèi	名	place; position
19 停	tíng	动	stop
20 祝	zhù	动	wish
21 平安	píng'ān	形	safe

三 注释 Notes

(一)"把"字句（1）

"把"字句是介词"把"及其宾语在句子中作状语的动词谓语句。"把"字句表达通过动作使某确定事物（"把"的宾语）发生某种变化或产生某种结果。这种变化或结果一般是位置的移动、从属关系的转移或形态的变化等。

结构形式是:（主语+）把+宾语+动词+补语+宾语（+了）

"把" sentence is a sentence with a verbal predicate, in which the preposition "把" and its object jointly function as an adverbial. A "把" sentence is used to indicate the change or result brought about by a certain thing (the object of "把") through an action. The change or result usually involves a change in position, a transfer of ownership or a change of state, etc.

The structure is: (subject +) 把 + object + verb + complement + object（+ 了）

例如：For example:

1. 把这些行李放到后备箱里去吧。
2. 把这个小箱子放在座位上去吧
3. 注意别把什么东西落车上了。

（二）放不下

句中"放不下"的意思是：地方小，不能容纳。它的反义词是"放得下"。例如：

“放不下” in this sentence means the space is too small for something. Its antonym is “放得下”. For example:

A：把这三个大箱子放进后备箱里，放得下放不下？

B：放不下 / 放得下。

四 练习 Exercises

（一）朗读下列发音相近的词语 Read aloud the following words with similar pronunciation

dāchéng 搭乘	dáchéng 达成	píng'ān 平安	pínfán 频繁
fàng xià 放 下	fàng jià 放 假	qíngkuàng 情况	qīngkuáng 轻狂
qiānwàn 千万	jiànwàng 健忘	jìn lì 尽力	jīnglì 精力

（二）替换并朗读 Replace and read aloud

1. 把行李放到后备箱里去吧。

椅子	教室里
背包	桌子下面
这些东西	院子里
这些书	书架上
衣服	衣柜里
护照	抽屉里

2. 你看放得下放不下？

坐　吃　装　睡　写　画

请你说出：说话人让你“看”什么？

（饭菜　教室　箱子　衣柜　书架　房间　本子　纸　床）

（三）**选词填空并朗读下列句子** Choose the appropriate words to fill in the blanks and read aloud the following sentences

下　就　把　马上　平安　什么

1. A：是您要的车吧，车已经到您楼下了。
   B：我们________下去。
2. A：把这些行李放到后备箱里去吧。这些箱子放得下放不下？放不下的话，只把这两个大箱子放进后备箱里，把这个小箱子放到座位上去吧。
   B：没问题，都放得________。
3. 要看交通情况，不堵车的话，大概 40 多分钟________到了。
4. A：师傅，您不用着急，要注意安全。
   B：放心吧，干我们这一行的，________时候都得把安全放在第一位。安全第一嘛。
5. 我把车停在 8 号门口儿。下车吧，注意别________什么东西落在车上了。祝你们一路________！

（四）**把下列词语组成"把"字句，然后大声读 5 遍** Make "把" sentences using the following words and read them aloud five times

例：我　车　把　了　在　8 号　门口儿　停→我把车停在 8 号门口儿了。

1. 客人　我　机场　了　把　送　到→
   ____。
2. 把　他　车　公寓楼　下面　了　在　停→
   ____。
3. 花　阳台　你　盆　去　到　上　吧　把　放　这→
   ____。
4. 发给　把　拍　的　你　在　长城　上　照片　我　吧→
   ____。

5. 我 你 里 到 视频 把 拍 的 发 手机 了 昨天→

____。

6. 这 篇 英文 我 翻译 把 课文 成了 中文/法文/日文→

____。

（五）边做边说，和同学一起练习“把”字句 Do and say, and then practice “把” sentences with your classmates

例如：A：请你把书放在课桌上。

B：（按A说的做后）我已经把书放在课桌上了。

1. A：请你把书打开。

B：____。

2. A：请你把书翻到第16页。

B：____。

3. A：请你把课文读一遍。

B：____。

4. A：请你把“出租车”翻译成英语。

B：____。

5. A：请你把书合上。

B：____。

6. A：请你把书放到书包里去。

B：____。

（六）你是A，请你向B提问 Supposing you are A, ask B questions

1. A：____？

B：来中国以后我常搭乘出租车。

2. A：____？

B：这里搭乘出租车比较方便。

3. A：____？

B：我觉得不太贵。

4. A：____？

B：我住的这个城市出租车不太多。

5. A：____？

B：在我们国家我不常搭乘出租车。

（七）**根据实际情况回答问题** Answer the questions according to your actual situations

1. 你们国家城市交通怎么样？堵车不堵车？
2. 来中国后，你常坐什么车？
3. 你现在住的城市交通方便不方便？
4. 你搭乘过出租车吗？
5. 你对司机的服务满意吗？
6. 你遇到过什么问题没有？

（八）**和同学一起表演课文** Act out the text with your classmates

（九）**读后说** Read the passage and say it

我要和同学一起坐飞机去西藏旅行。昨天我用"滴滴打车"约了一辆车。今天司机师傅提前十分钟就把车开到了我们公寓楼下。听到师傅叫我们，我们马上就下楼了。师傅把我们的箱子放进了后备箱，我把一个小箱子放在了座位上。幸运的是，路上没堵车，大概40分钟我们就到了机场。师傅把车停在了8号门口儿，我们把行李拿了下来。师傅祝我们一路平安，我们谢过师傅，就进了机场。

（十）**怎么表达** How to express

tí xǐng
提 醒 a reminder

Xiǎoxīn bié gǎnmào le!
1. 小心 别 感冒 了！

Don't catch a cold!

Kǎoshì de shíhou, qiānwàn bié jǐnzhāng.
2. 考试的时候，千万别紧张。

Don't be nervous when you take an exam.

Nǐ qiānwàn búyào dàyi.
3. 你千万不要大意。

Do be careful.

（十一）朗读中国经典诗词，请注意语音语调 Read aloud the classic Chinese poem and pay attention to the pronunciation and intonation

Huánghè Lóu Sòng Mèng Hàorán zhī Guǎnglíng
黄鹤楼送孟浩然之广陵

[Táng] Lǐ Bái
［唐］李白（701—762）

Gùrén xī cí Huánghè Lóu, yānhuā Sānyuè xià Yáng Zhōu.
故人西辞黄鹤楼，烟花三月下扬州。

Gū fān yuǎn yǐng bìkōng jìn, wéi jiàn Cháng Jiāng tiānjì liú.
孤帆远影碧空尽，唯见长江天际流。

（十二）请欣赏下列著名的词句 Please enjoy the following famous saying

Bú pà màn, jiù pà zhàn.
不怕慢，就怕站。

It's better to move ahead slowly than just marking time.

Dì-sānshíbā kè Wèi sòng wàimài de xiǎo gē diǎn zàn

第三十八课 为送外卖的小哥点赞

Lesson 38 Give the take-out delivery boy a like

一 课文 Text

A：最近怎么样？看样子你过得很好嘛。

B：是，我过得非常好。我对这里的一切都感兴趣，最近我又对一件事儿产生了兴趣，你知道是什么吗？

A：你不说我怎么知道，是什么事儿？

B：叫外卖。

A：是吗？

B：是啊。我觉得半夜的外卖服务，好极了。

A：你怎么半夜还叫外卖呀？

B：因为我一到半夜就饿，所以常常叫外卖。

A：半夜还有外卖呀？

B：有啊。我叫完外卖，不一会儿，送外卖的小哥就到了。他知道我是外国人，汉语说得不好，所以一边轻轻地敲门，一边小声地说："外卖。"我一开门，他就伸手把饭盒递过来，我还没来得及说谢谢呢，他说了句："给个好评啊。"就走了。

A：什么意思呀？

B：开始我也不懂是什么意思，问了中国同学才明白，他是要我给他点个赞。

A：真有意思。

B：我看他那么急，以后再来，就对他说，放门口儿吧！他一听，把饭盒放下就跑了。

A：他们很辛苦。

B：是。因为看他工作努力、服务热心，所以我常常想给他们点儿小费。一次，我给一个小哥一百元小费，谁知道，他很认真地对我说："我们这儿不兴这个。"

A：真的吗？

B：我听他这么说，感到有点儿惭愧，好像玷污了一颗纯洁的心。因为在我们国家，去饭店吃饭必须给服务员小费。可在这儿就不用给。

A：国情不同嘛。

B：你说得也对。可是，我总想向他们表示一下感激的心情。

二 生词 New Words

1 为	wèi	介	for
2 外卖	wàimài	名	take-out
3 点赞	diǎn zàn	动	give sb. a like/thumbs-up
4 看样子	kàn yàngzi		it looks as if
5 一切	yíqiè	代	all; every; everything
6 感	gǎn	动	feel
7 兴趣	xìngqù	名	interest
8 产生	chǎnshēng	动	engender
9 半夜	bànyè	名	midnight

10	轻	qīng	形	gentle
11	小声	xiǎo shēng		in a low voice
12	伸手	shēn shǒu	动	stretch out one's hand
13	递	dì	动	give; pass
14	来得及	láidejí	动	there's still time; be able to do sth. in time
	来不及	láibují	动	it's too late (to do sth.); there's not enough time (to do sth.)
15	好评	hǎopíng	名	favorable comment
16	明白	míngbai	动、形	understand; clear
17	热心	rèxīn	形	warm-hearted; enthusiastic
	心	xīn	名	heart; mind
18	小费	xiǎofèi	名	tip; gratuity
19	兴	xīng	动	prevail; be in vogue
20	感到	gǎndào	动	feel
21	玷污	diànwū	动	sully
22	颗	kē	量	*a measure word for anything small and roundish*
23	纯洁	chúnjié	形	pure
24	国情	guóqíng	名	national condition
25	总	zǒng	副	always
26	表示	biǎoshì	动	express; show
27	感激	gǎnjī	动	feel grateful
28	心情	xīnqíng	名	state of mind

三 注释 Notes

（一）一……就……

“一……就……”可以表示后一动作紧跟着前一动作发生。例如：

“一……就……” indicates the latter action immediately follows the previous one. For example:

1. 我一到星期六就去学书法。
2. 他一到上海就给我来了电话。
3. 他一毕业就来他们国家驻华使馆工作了。

“一……就……”也表示前一动作是条件和原因，后一动作是结果。例如：

“一……就……” also indicates the previous action is the condition and reason, and the latter action is the result. For example:

1. 他一听就知道我是外国人。
2. 我一感冒就发烧。
3. 她一喝酒就脸红。

（二）谁知道

“谁知道”的意思是：没想到。

“谁知道” means “unexpectedly”.

（三）可

句中的“可”跟“可是”一样，都表示转折，意思是：但是。

“可” in the sentence equals to “可是”, both of which indicate transition, meaning “but”.

四 练习 Exercises

（一）朗读 Read aloud

1. 朗读下列发音相近的词语 Read aloud the following words with similar pronunciation

xìngqù	xīngqī	xiǎofèi	xiāofèi
兴趣	星期	小费	消费

qiāo mén 敲 门	qiàomén 窍门	gǎnjī 感激	gǎn jí 赶 集
guóqíng 国情	guóqìng 国庆	bù tóng 不 同	bù tōng 不 通

2. 朗读下列词组 Read the following phrases aloud

好极了	棒极了	渴极了	饿极了	多极了
忙极了	快极了	慢极了	累极了	困极了
高兴极了	漂亮极了	舒服极了	方便极了	

看样子你过得很好　看样子你心情不错　看样子你身体很棒

看样子她不太高兴　看样子她有什么心事　看样子她有话要对我说

（二）**选词填空并朗读下列句子** Choose the appropriate words to fill in the blanks and read aloud the following sentences

极　对　必须　才　惭愧　兴　一边　就

1. A：你最近过得怎么样？
   B：我过得非常好。最近我又________一件事儿产生了兴趣，你知道是什么吗？
2. A：你不说我怎么知道，是什么事儿？
   B：我觉得半夜的外卖服务，好________了。
3. A：你怎么半夜还叫外卖啊？
   B：因为我一到半夜________饿，所以常常叫外卖。
4. 我叫完外卖，不一会儿，送外卖的小哥就到了。他知道我是外国人，汉语说得不好，所以一边轻轻地敲门，________小声地说：“外卖。”我一开门，他就伸手把饭盒递过来，我还没来得及说谢谢呢，他说了句：“给个好评啊。”就走了。
5. 开始我也不懂是什么意思，问了中国同学________明白。他是要我给他点个赞。
6. 因为看他工作努力、服务热心，所以我常常想给他们点儿小费。

一次，我给一个小哥一百元小费，谁知道，他很认真地对我说：“我们这儿不________这个。”

7. 我听他这么说，感到有点儿________，好像玷污了一颗纯洁的心。

8. 因为在我们国家，去饭店吃饭________给服务员小费。可在这儿就不用给。

（三）将 A、B 两列连线，组成正确的句子，然后朗读 Match A with B to make correct sentences and read them aloud

1. “一……就……”

A	B
一到半夜	就把鞋脱了。
我一上课	就兴奋（xīngfèn, excited）得睡不着觉。
我一到周末	我就饿得想吃东西。
中午我一下课	就困得不行。
他一进屋	就去食堂吃饭。
我一喝咖啡	就想跟国内的同学通话。

2. “一边……一边……”

A	B
她在湖边一边散步	一边唱，非常快乐。
我一边想	一边笑。
我喜欢一边听音乐	一边聊天儿。
她一边说	一边听着音乐。
她们一边跳	一边写，才写了五个句子。
她们一边喝着咖啡	一边写 / 做作业。

（四）用“可能”“看样子”填空 Fill in the blanks with “可能” or “看样子”

例：（1）他没来，可能生病了。

（2）他的脸很红，看样子又喝酒了。

1. 今天温度（wēndù, temperature）这么高，不________下雪。

2. 他________比我大一岁。
3. 这么晚还没回来，他________有什么事了。
4. ________他有点儿不高兴。
5. 快八点了，________我们今天又要迟到了。
6. 我________把书忘教室里了。

（五）你是 A，请你向 B 提问 Supposing you are A, ask B questions

1. A：________________________________？
   B：我有点儿不舒服。
2. A：________________________________？
   B：我想学太极拳。
3. A：________________________________？
   B：我下星期要去上海。
4. A：________________________________？
   B：我去给一个外贸代表团当翻译。
5. A：________________________________？
   B：我坐高铁去。
6. A：________________________________？
   B：假期我想去南方旅行。

（六）根据实际情况回答问题 Answer the questions according to your actual situations

1. 说说你对什么比较 / 很 / 不感兴趣？
2. 你现在会叫外卖吗？你叫没叫过外卖？
3. 你会不会弹钢琴（gāngqín, piano）/ 拉小提琴（xiǎotíqín, violin）？
4. 你对画画儿有没有兴趣？
5. 你跟中国人聊过天儿吗？
6. 你想没想过和中国人聊聊天儿？

（七）请说说你对以下哪个事情感兴趣 Which of the following are you interested in

例如：A：你对书法感兴趣吗？
　　　B：我对书法很 / 比较 / 不 / 一点儿也不感兴趣。

爬山	玩儿游戏	武术	漫画	逛超市/书店/夜市		
太极拳/剑	跳舞	唱歌	摄影	上网	茶道	健美操
听音乐	做中国菜	中医	滑雪	冲浪	足球	练瑜伽

（**提示**：不认识的词请问百度/谷歌/中国朋友或同学。）

（**Reminder:** Search on Baidu/Google or ask your Chinese friends/classmates for the words you don't know.）

（八）和同学一起表演课文 Act out the text with your classmates

（九）读后说 Read the passage and say it

来中国以后，我对很多事情都产生了兴趣。最近，我喜欢叫外卖。因为一到晚上十点多，我就饿，所以常常叫外卖。送外卖的小哥一到我门口，就小声说着："301，外卖。"我一开门，他马上就把我的饭盒递了过来，我还来不及说声"谢谢"呢，他就走了。一边走还一边说："给个好评啊。"

我看他们很辛苦，就想给他们点儿小费。一次，我拿出一百块钱递给一个小哥，想表达我感激的心情。可是他却对我说："我们这儿不兴这个。"我把钱收起来后，突然感到有点儿惭愧。我想，自己是不是太把钱当回事儿了。因为在我们国家，去饭店吃饭必须给服务员小费。

这件事让我明白，国情不同，很多人和事也是不同的。

（十）怎么表达 How to express

cánkuì
惭愧　being ashamed

Wǒ shēn gǎn cánkuì.
1. 我 深 感 惭愧。

I feel deeply ashamed.

Wǒ méi kǎo jígé,　hěn cánkuì.
2. 我 没 考及格，很 惭愧。

I'm ashamed that I failed the exam.

Gōngzuò méi zuòhǎo, wǒ hěn cánkuì.
3. 工作 没 做好，我 很 惭愧。

I'm ashamed that I didn't do my job well.

（十一）朗读中国经典诗词，请注意语音语调 Read aloud the classic Chinese poem and pay attention to the pronunciation and intonation

Jiāng Shàng Yúzhě
江 上 渔者

[Sòng] Fàn Zhòngyān
[宋] 范 仲淹 （989—1052）

Jiāng shàng wǎnglái rén, dàn ài lúyú měi.
江 上 往来 人，但 爱 鲈 鱼 美。

Jūn kàn yí yè zhōu, chūmò fēngbō lǐ.
君 看 一 叶 舟，出没 风波 里。

（十二）请欣赏下列著名的词句 Please enjoy the following famous saying

Xué rú nìshuǐ-xíngzhōu, bújìn-zétuì.
学如 逆水行舟，不进则退。

Learning is like rowing upstream; if you do not try to advance, you will drop back.

Dì-sānshíjiǔ kè

第三十九课 Lesson 39

Nǐ de zuòpǐn bèi fàng zài zhǎnlǎn chúchuāng li le

你的作品被放在展览橱窗里了

Your work is in the show window

一 课文 Text

（一）你的作品被放在展览橱窗里了

兰笛：罗兰，告诉你一个好消息。

罗兰：什么好消息？

兰笛：你的作品被放进展览橱窗里展出了。

罗兰：作品？什么作品？

兰笛：就是你画的画儿，写的字呀。

罗兰：是吗？你怎么知道的？

兰笛：（拿手机）你看，我都把它给你拍下来了。

罗兰：这是在哪儿呀？

兰笛：就是校园里的展览橱窗啊。

罗兰：啊，真不好意思。

兰笛：你才学了不到半年啊，就画得这么好，真不简单！

罗兰：哪里，可能是老师为了鼓励我们，才展出的吧。你常看展览橱窗啊？

兰笛：我看是看，但只是看看图片。因为除了图片以外，里面的文章我还看不懂。

罗兰：我也是，从那儿过的时候，就是浏览一下图片。

（二）肚子突然疼起来了

A：哎哟……

B：你怎么了？

A：我肚子突然疼起来了。

B：厉害吗？要不要上医院？

A：我有点儿恶心，很难受，想吐。

B：想吐就吐出来吧，吐出来可能就舒服了。

（A 呕吐了）

B：快！喝口水漱漱嘴。你可能是吃得不合适了，是不是中午吃火锅吃的？

A：啊，可能吧。

（过了一会儿）

B：怎么样？现在好点儿了吗？

A：好多了。可能是吃得太多太杂了。

B：吐出来就舒服了，是不是？肚子还疼吗？

A：是，现在肚子一点儿也不疼了。

B：没事儿就好，把我吓了一跳。

二 生词 New Words

1 作品	zuòpǐn	名	work
2 被	bèi	介	(*used in a passive sentence to introduce the agent*) by
3 展览	zhǎnlǎn	动	exhibit
4 橱窗	chúchuāng	名	show window
5 消息	xiāoxi	名	news

6	展出	zhǎnchū	动	exhibit
7	鼓励	gǔlì	动	encourage
8	除了	chúle	介	except
9	以外	yǐwài	名	other than
10	文章	wénzhāng	名	article
11	浏览	liúlǎn	动	glance over; browse
12	肚子	dùzi	名	tummy; stomach; belly
13	突然	tūrán	形	suddenly
14	疼	téng	形	pain; ache
15	哎哟	āiyō	叹	(*expressing astonishment, pain or pity*) ow
16	医院	yīyuàn	名	hospital
17	恶心	ěxin	形	(feel) nauseated
18	吐	tù	动	vomit
	呕吐	ǒutù	动	throw up; vomit
19	难受	nánshòu	形	(feel) uncomfortable
20	出来	chū lái	动	*used after a verb to indicate the direction of motion from inside*
21	漱嘴	shù zuǐ	动	gargle
	漱	shù	动	gargle
22	火锅	huǒguō	名	hot pot
23	杂	zá	形	sundry; mixed
24	没事儿	méi shìr	动	that's all right; never mind
25	吓	xià	动	frighten
26	跳	tiào	动	jump

三 注释 Notes

(一)“被”字句

“被”及其宾语作状语来表示被动意义的动词谓语句。例如：

The “被” and its object are used as an adverbial to express the passive voice. For example:

他被大家选为班长了。

口语中，一般用介词“让”“叫”“给”来替代“被”。用“让”“叫”时，后边必须有宾语（施事者）。例如：

In spoken Chinese, “被” is often replaced by prepositions such as “让”, “叫” and “给”. “让” and “叫” must be followed by an object (agent). For example:

1. 我的电动车叫麦克骑去了。
2. 他的腿让自行车撞伤了。

(二) 除了……以外

介词“除了”表示所说的不计算在内，后面常加“以外”。例如：

The preposition “除了” means “not including; apart from; besides.” It is often followed by “以外”. For example:

1. 除了图片以外，里面的文章我还看不懂。
2. 我们班除了山本以外，都是第一次来中国。

(三) 看是看

“看是看”里“是”前后用相同的名词、形容词或动词，含有“虽然”的意思。例如：

In the phrase “看是看”, which means “although”, there must be the same nouns, adjectives or verbs before and after “是”. For example:

1. 文章是好文章，就是有点儿长。
2. 我看是看了，但是没看懂。
3. 这个手机好是好，就是太贵了，我买不起。

四 练习 Exercises

（一）朗读下列发音相近的词语 Read aloud the following words with similar pronunciation

gàosu 告诉	gāosù 高速	xiāoxi 消息	xiǎo xī 小溪
gǔlì 鼓励	gūlì 孤立	zhǎnchū 展出	chǎnchū 产出
héshì 合适	hé shí 何时	dùzi 肚子	tùzi 兔子

（二）替换并朗读 Replace and read aloud

1. 我都把它<u>拍</u>下来了。

   画　写　复印（fùyìn, xerox）
   记　录
   下载（xiàzài, download）

2. 她才学了不到半年哪，
   就<u>画</u>得这么好，真不简单！

   学　写　说
   跳　打　唱

3. A：你怎么了？
   B：我<u>肚子</u>有点儿疼。

   头　腿　牙　手　脚

4. A：现在还<u>疼</u>吗？
   B：一点儿也 / 都不<u>疼</u>了。

   渴　饿　难受
   热　冷

请你说说：她学 / 写 / 说 / 跳 / 打 / 唱的可能是什么？

（三）**选词填空并朗读下列句子** Choose the appropriate words to fill in the blanks and read aloud the following sentences

得　为了　是　过　下来　到

1. 罗兰，告诉你一个好消息。你的作品被放________展览橱窗里展出了。
2. 你看，我都把它给你拍________了。
3. 你才学了不到半年啊，就画________这么好，真不简单！
4. 哪里，可能是老师________鼓励我们，才展出的吧。
5. 这个橱窗我看________看，但只是看看图片。因为除了图片以外，里面的文章我还看不懂。
6. 我也是，从那儿________的时候，就是浏览一下图片。

了　起来　不　合适　得　就

1. A：哎哟……我的肚子突然疼________了。
   B：厉害吗？要不要去医院？
2. A：我有点儿恶心，很难受，想吐。
   B：想吐________吐出来吧，吐出来可能就舒服了
3. 快！喝口水漱漱嘴。你可能是吃得不________了，是不是中午吃火锅吃的？
4. A：怎么样？现在好点儿了吗？
   B：好多________。
5. 可能是吃________太多太杂了。
6. 现在肚子一点儿也________疼了。

（四）将 A、B 两列连线，组成正确的句子，然后朗读 Match A with B to make correct sentences and read them aloud

1.“被”

A	B
他的作文	被我们选为班长了。
爱德华的腿	被小偷儿偷走了。
那个茶杯	被警察抓住了。
她	被老师读给我们听了。
我的手机	被我不小心摔破了。
那个小偷儿	被自行车撞了一下。

2.“A 是 A”

A	B
他去是去，	可是因为不用，忘得差不多了。
我听是听了，	但是太贵了。
日语我学是学过，	但不跟我们一起去，他想自己一个人去。
东西好是好，	但是没听懂。
这篇课文长是长，	但是每天都过得很快乐。
我忙是忙了点儿，	但是生词不多，也很有意思，我看懂了。

请你用“A 是 A”说一个句子。

（五）请你用“把”字句说出下列句子，然后大声读一读 Please use “把” sentences to rewrite the following sentences and then read them aloud

例：他被自行车撞倒了→自行车把他撞倒了。

1. 我的电动车让朋友借去了→

____。

2. 手机让我摔坏了→

____。

3. 树叶都被大风刮下来了→

____。

4. 他的病让大夫治好了→

____。

5. 我的箱子叫服务员提到楼上去了→

____。

6. 她画的这张画儿被我拍下来了→

____。

（六）回答课文的问题 Answer the questions about the text

1. 兰笛告诉罗兰一个什么消息？
2. 兰笛在哪儿看到的？
3. 罗兰知道这个消息吗？
4. 兰笛是怎么给罗兰看的？
5. 罗兰为什么觉得不好意思？
6. 罗兰学习书法和画画儿多长时间了？

（七）你是 A，请你向 B 提问 Supposing you are A, ask B questions

1. A：____？

B：吃过午饭，我突然觉得肚子疼。

2. A：____？

B：我没有去医院，肚子疼得去不了医院。

3. A：____？

B：后来就吐了。

4. A：____？

B：吐了以后，就觉得好多了。

5. A：____？

B：我想是吃东西太多，也太杂了。

6. A：____？

B：谢谢你。

（八）你是B，请用“除了……以外”回答A的问题 Suppose you are B and answer A's questions using “除了……以外”

1. A：你们班都有哪些国家的同学？
   B：____。
2. A：中餐你都喜欢吃什么？
   B：____。
3. A：来中国后你都去过什么地方？
   B：____。
4. A：你常去图书馆借书吗？
   B：____。
5. A：你最喜欢什么体育运动？
   B：____。
6. A：昨天有多少同学参加你的生日晚会？
   B：____。

（九）根据实际情况回答问题 Answer the questions according to your actual situations

1. 你们学校有没有展览橱窗？
2. 展览橱窗里都展览什么？你常看吗？
3. 口语课的课文你现在看得懂看不懂？
4. 你常常利用“百度”或“谷歌”学习汉语吗？
5. 你有没有突然感觉不舒服的时候？
6. 来中国后，你得过病没有？

（十）和同学一起表演课文 Act out the text with your classmates

（十一）读后说 Read the passage and say it

今天，兰笛告诉我一个消息。她说我画的一张画儿和写的一幅字被老师放进展览橱窗里展出了。我有点儿不相信，她就把手机拍下来的照片给我看，我看了以后觉得很不好意思。我自己觉得那幅字写得不好，画儿也画得不是很满意。可能是老师为了鼓励我们，才把这些字和画挂进了橱窗里去的。我想，我要坚持写下去、画下去，不为别的，只为让自己在中国的留学生活更丰富、更有意思。

（十二）怎么表达 How to express

gǎntàn
感叹 exclamation

Hǎo piàoliang de huàr ya!
1. 好 漂亮 的画儿呀！

What a beautiful picture!

Zhège gēr tài hǎotīng le.
2. 这个歌儿太好听了。

This song is so beautiful.

Zhèr de fēngjǐng duō měi ya!
3. 这儿的风景多美呀！

What beautiful scenery it is!

（十三）朗读中国经典诗词，请注意语音语调 Read aloud the classic Chinese poem and pay attention to the pronunciation and intonation

Yǒng Liǔ
咏柳

[Táng] Hè Zhīzhāng
［唐］贺 知章（659—744）

Bìyù zhuāng chéng yí shù gāo, wàn tiáo chuí xià lǜ sī tāo.
碧玉妆成一树高，万条垂下绿丝绦。
Bù zhī xì yè shuí cáichū, Èryuè chūnfēng sì jiǎndāo.
不知细叶谁裁出，二月春风似剪刀。

（十四）请欣赏下列著名的词句 Please enjoy the following famous saying

Jūnzǐ zhī jiāo dàn rú shuǐ.
君子之交淡如水。

Friends agree best at a distance.

Dì-sìshí kè　　Míngtiān dào de liǎo dào bu liǎo

第四十课　明天 到得了到不了

Lesson 40　Will it arrive tomorrow?

一　课文 Text

（在快递服务公司）

A：我寄个快件。

B：你寄什么东西？

A：我寄一件毛衣、一盒中成药、两本书，还有一个优盘。

B：往哪儿寄？

A：上海。

B：我先给你包装一下，装这个塑料袋里行吗？

A：可以。要填包裹单吗？

B：你手机里有收件人的姓名、地址、手机号吗？

A：有。

B：让我用手机扫（描）一下就可以了，好了。

A：真方便！多少钱？

B：十八块。

A：明天到得了到不了？

B：明天可能到不了，后天或大后天对方才能收到。

二 生词 New Words

1	了	liǎo	动	(*used in conjunction with* "得" *or* "不" *after a verb*) can
2	寄	jì	动	send
3	快件	kuàijiàn	名	express delivery luggage, goods or mail
4	件	jiàn	量	*a measure word for clothing, furniture, luggage, etc.*
5	毛衣	máoyī	名	sweater
6	中成药	zhōngchéngyào	名	Chinese patent medicine
7	优盘	yōupán	名	USB flash drive
8	包装	bāozhuāng	动	wrap sth. up
	装	zhuāng	动	put in
9	塑料	sùliào	名	plastic
10	袋	dài	名	bag
11	包裹	bāoguǒ	名	parcel
12	单	dān	名	list; bill
13	收件	shōujiàn	动	receive (a mail, parcel, etc.)
14	地址	dìzhǐ	名	address
15	扫(描)	sǎo (miáo)	动	scan
16	后天	hòutiān	名	the day after tomorrow
	大后天	dàhòutiān	名	three days from now
17	对方	duìfāng	名	other side; other party

三 注释 Notes

可能补语

可能补语表示主客观条件能否允许进行某种动作或实现某种结果和变化。

Complement of potentiality indicates whether the subjective and objective conditions allow an action to be performed, or a result or change to be realized.

1. 动词 + 得 / 不 + 结果补语 / 趋向补语

Verb + 得 / 不 + result complement / complement of direction

例如：For example:

（1）这个快件明天到得了到不了？

（2）你听得见我的声音吗？

（3）不戴眼镜你看得见吗？

2. 动词 + 得 / 不 + 了（liǎo）：表示动作能否发生或完成

Verb + 得 / 不 + 了 (liǎo): It indicates whether an action can be performed or completed

（1）表示动作行为能否发生。例如：

It indicates whether an action can be performed, For example:

① A：明天爬山，你去得了吗？

B：我明天有朋友来，去不了。

② A：他自己走得了吗？

B：他脚受伤了，自己走不了。

（2）表示动作行为能否完成（“了”有“完”的意思）。例如：

It indicates whether an action can be completed (“ 了 ” means “to finish”). For example:

① A：这些包子你吃得了吃不了？

B：太多了，我吃不了。

② 今天的作业不多，用不了一个小时就做完了。

四 练习 Exercises

（一）朗读 Read aloud

1. 朗读下列发音相近的词语 Read aloud the following words with similar pronunciation

kuàijiàn 快件	kuān xiàn 宽 限	máoyī 毛衣	màoyì 贸易
dìfang 地方	dīfáng 提防	shōudào 收到	shūbào 书报
dìzhǐ 地址	dìzhì 地质	xìnxī 信息	xīnxǐ 欣喜

2. 朗读下列词组并组成问句 Read aloud the following phrases and make interrogative sentences

到得了到不了　　去得了去不了　　来得了来不了

喝得了喝不了　　吃得了吃不了　　拿得了拿不了

请你用每个词组说一个问句。

Please make an interrogative sentence using each phrase.

（二）替换并朗读 Replace and read aloud

1. 我寄（一）个快件。

一本词典　　两本书
一个包裹　　三盒中药

2. A：寄到什么地方 / 哪儿？
   B：寄到上海。

北京　　广州　　天津
深圳　　台北　　香港

3. A：明天到得了到不了？
   B：明天到不了。

七点钟　　来　　一个小时　　做
四个包子　　吃　　中午　　取
星期六　　去
两杯啤酒（píjiǔ, beer）　　喝

（三）选词填空并朗读下列句子 Choose the appropriate words to fill in the blanks and read aloud the following sentences

才　　件　　一下　　了　　就

1. A：你要寄什么东西？
   B：我寄一________毛衣、一盒中成药、两本书，还有一个优盘。
2. 我先给你包装________，装这个塑料袋里行吗？
3. 你手机里有收件人的姓名、地址、手机号吗？我用手机扫（描）一下________可以了，不用填包裹单。
4. A：明天到得________到不________？
   B：明天可能到不了，后天或大后天对方________能收到。

（四）和同学一起练习以下会话 Practice the following conversations with your classmates

1. A：丹尼丝爬的那座山有多高？
   B：大概有五百多米。
   A：你爬得上去吗？
   B：我没爬过，不知道爬得上去爬不上去。
   A：这个周末我们也去爬爬怎么样？
   B：不行，我腿疼，爬不了。

2. A：咱们八点出发，九点到得了吗？
   B：到得了。高铁时速（shísù, speed per hour）三百多公里呢。
   A：今天去，星期日晚上回得来吗？
   B：没问题，回得来。
   A：要是买不到车票呢？
   B：高铁的车次（chēcì, train number）很多，票好买，肯定买得到。

3. A：明天早上六点钟你起得来吗？
   B：六点太早了，我起不来。

A：今晚早点儿睡，早睡的话起得来。

B：那也不行，早睡我睡不着。

4. A：要四十个饺子，咱们吃得了吃不了？

B：四十个？我只能吃十几个，你吃得了吗？

A：我吃得了。一瓶啤酒你喝得了喝不了？

B：喝不了，我只能喝一杯。

（五）**请你根据画线部分提问** Please ask questions about the underlined parts

例如：下午我要去寄一个快件。→ 下午你要做什么？

1. 我要往我们国内寄一个包裹。→

______________________________？

2. 包裹里有一件毛衣、两本书和一个优盘。→

______________________________？

3. 我给一个朋友寄。→

______________________________？

4. 这些东西要用塑料袋包装一下。→

______________________________？

5. 营业员扫一下我手机就可以了。→

______________________________？

6. 这个快件一周后才能到。→

______________________________？

（六）**根据实际情况回答问题** Answer the questions according to your actual situations

1. 你寄过快递没有？
2. 你往哪里寄过快递？
3. 寄的什么东西？
4. 课堂上老师说的话你都听得懂吗？
5. 现在口语课的课文你读得了读不了？
6. 遇到生词和不认识的字你是怎么做的？

（七）和同学一起表演课文 Act out the text with your classmates

（八）读后说 Read the passage and say it

今天我去寄快递的地方，给上海的朋友寄一个快件。营业员问我寄的什么东西，我说是一件毛衣、一盒中成药、两本书和一个优盘。他说："给你包装一下吧。装一个塑料袋里，你看行吗？"我说："可以，非常好。"我问他要不要填包裹单，他说我手机里要是有对方的姓名、地址和手机号的话，用手机扫一下就可以了，非常方便。我问他明天到得了到不了，他说明天可能到不了，后天或大后天才能到。

（九）怎么表达 How to express

fā shì
发誓 pledge; swear

Wǒ fā shì bú zài chōu yān le.
1. 我发誓不再抽烟了。
I swear off smoking from now.

Wǒ fā shì zài yě bù chídào le.
2. 我发誓再也不迟到了。
I promise I will not be late again.

（十）朗读中国经典诗词，请注意语音语调 Read aloud the classic Chinese poem and pay attention to the pronunciation and intonation

Wàng Lú Shān Pùbù
望庐山瀑布

[Táng] Lǐ Bái
[唐] 李白（701—762）

Rì zhào xiānglú shēng zǐ yān, yáo kàn pùbù guà qián chuān.
日照香炉生紫烟，遥看瀑布挂前川。
Fēi liú zhí xià sānqiān chǐ, yí shì Yín Hé luò jiǔtiān.
飞流直下三千尺，疑是银河落九天。

（十一）请欣赏下列著名的词句 Please enjoy the following famous saying

Wēn gù ér zhī xīn.

温故而知新。

Gain new knowledge by reviewing the old.

Dì-sìshíyī kè Tā yǒu yì kē shànliáng de xīn
第四十一课 她有一颗善良的心
Lesson 41 She is kind-hearted

一 课文 Text

（安丽和爱琳在谈话）

爱琳：昨天你去哪儿了？我给你打手机你没接，发短信，你也不回。

安丽：对不起，你来电话的时候，我把手机调成静音了，听不见。

爱琳：为什么要调成静音啊？

安丽：因为那时候我正在按摩呢。

爱琳：按摩？在哪儿按摩？

安丽：在一家盲人按摩院。

爱琳：盲人按摩，我只听说过，但从来没见过，我也从来没做过按摩。

安丽：我是上网找到的。因为我想了解中国残疾人事业的情况。

爱琳：残疾人事业？你怎么对残疾人事业这么关心？

安丽：因为我非常同情残疾人。

爱琳：是吗？你的心真好。

安丽：哪里，因为我姐姐就是残疾人。

爱琳：啊！是吗？

安丽：是。姐姐小时候，被汽车撞了一下，成了残疾人。所以我对残疾人事业特别关心。你知道我读的什么专业吗?

爱琳：什么专业?

安丽：特殊教育专业。

爱琳：什么是特殊教育专业?

安丽：就是对残疾人进行教育的专业。

爱琳：我真没想到，你学的是这个专业。

安丽：我来这里留学，也是想了解这个大学特殊教育专业的情况。

爱琳：我们大学也有特殊教育专业?

安丽：有啊！我的朋友圈里，有不少这个专业的同学。认识她们以后，我觉得她们甘愿从事残疾人教育事业，可爱、可敬。

爱琳：啊，是这样啊。

安丽：我认识的残疾人，也一样可敬。就说给我按摩的盲人按摩师吧。她虽然是盲人，但非常善良，而且也非常专业。你不用说你哪儿不舒服，她用手一摸就知道了。

爱琳：有那么夸张吗?

安丽：不信你去试试就知道了。她说，人身上不舒服的地方，肌肉是僵硬的。

爱琳：听你这么一说，我真想去试试。

安丽：她对顾客的关爱，也让我感动。昨天她还对我说，不能太瘦了，为了健康，要增加营养。我听了心里暖暖的。一个盲人按摩师对顾客这么关爱，说明她有一颗善良的心。

爱琳：真好。下次你也带我去看看吧。

安丽：没问题。

二 生词 New Words

1	善良	shànliáng	形	kind-hearted
2	接	jiē	动	answer; receive
3	短信	duǎnxìn	名	text message; short message
4	调	tiáo	动	set
5	静音	jìng yīn	动	mute
6	按摩	ànmó	动	massage
	按摩院	ànmóyuàn	名	massage parlor
	按摩师	ànmóshī	名	massagist
7	盲人	mángrén	名	blind person
8	残疾人	cánjírén	名	the disabled; the handicapped
	残疾	cánjí	名	disability
9	事业	shìyè	名	career
10	同情	tóngqíng	动	sympathize
11	撞	zhuàng	动	crash
12	特殊	tèshū	形	special
13	教育	jiàoyù	名、动	education; teach
14	甘愿	gānyuàn	动	(be) willing (to do sth.)
15	从事	cóngshì	动	work on; be occupied in
16	摸	mō	动	feel; touch
17	夸张	kuāzhāng	形	exaggerated
18	信	xìn	动	believe
19	肌肉	jīròu	名	muscle
20	僵硬	jiāngyìng	形	stiff; rigid

21 顾客	gùkè	名	customer
22 感动	gǎndòng	动、形	move; moved
23 瘦	shòu	形	thin
24 健康	jiànkāng	形	healthy
25 增加	zēngjiā	动	increase; add
26 营养	yíngyǎng	名	nutrition
27 暖	nuǎn	形	warm
28 说明	shuōmíng	动、名	explain; explanation

专名 Zhuānmíng Proper Noun

爱琳	Àilín	name of a person

三 注释 Notes

无关联词语复句

汉语口语通常只用语序来表示小句之间的语义联系，只要小句之间语义清楚，符合逻辑，一般可以不用关联词。但实际上小句之间隐含着一定的逻辑关系。

Spoken Chinese, usually only uses word order to indicate the semantic relationship between clauses. As long as the semantics between clauses are clear and logical, it is usually unnecessary to use connectives. However, in fact, there is a certain logical relation between the clauses.

1. 表示假设关系。例如：

It indicates a hypothetical circumstance. For example:

（1）不信你去试试就知道了。＝要是你不信，去试试就知道了。

（2）你去我就去。＝要是你去的话，我就去。

（3）下雨就不去了。＝要是下雨的话，就不去了。

2. 表示因果关系。例如：

It indicates a cause-effect relationship. For example:

（1）不小心把手机丢了。＝因为不小心，所以把手机丢了。

（2）不小心把杯子碰倒了。＝因为不小心，所以把杯子碰倒了。

四 练习 Exercises

（一）朗读 Read aloud

1. 朗读下列发音相近的词语 Read aloud the following words with similar pronunciation

shànliáng 善良	shànyǎng 赡养	jìng yīn 静音	jīngyīng 精英
gùkè 顾客	gōngkè 功课	tèjiào 特教	tèxiào 特效
zēngjiā 增加	chéng jiā 成家	jiàoyù 教育	jiàoyì 教益

2. 朗读下列词组 Read the following phrases aloud

玩儿手机	发短信	回电话	调静音
非常专业	非常舒服	非常夸张	非常清楚

3. 朗读下列句子 Read the following sentences aloud

我正在按摩呢。	他正在听歌呢。	我们正在上课呢。
我真没听说过。	我真没按摩过。	我真没参观过。
我真没见过。	我真没看过。	我真没算过。
一摸就知道了。	一说就清楚了。	一讲就懂了。
一学就会了。	一练就熟了。	一看就明白了。

不信你去试试就知道了。　　不信你去看看就知道了。

不信你尝尝就知道了。　　不信你去逛逛就知道了。

（二）**替换并朗读** Replace and read aloud

1\. 你来电话的时候，我正在<u>按摩</u>呢。

上课
学打太极拳
洗澡
睡觉
跟朋友聊天儿
地铁上

2\. 你这么一说，我真想去<u>试试</u>。

看看	参观参观
学学	按摩按摩
逛逛	体验体验

（三）**选词填空并朗读下列句子** Choose the appropriate words to fill in the blanks and read aloud the following sentences

怎么　让　所以　颗　从事　觉得　成　从来

1\. A：昨天你去哪儿了？我给你打手机你没接，发短信，你也不回。
　B：对不起，你来电话的时候，我把手机调________静音了。

2\. A：为什么要调成静音啊？
　B：因为那时候我正在盲人按摩院按摩呢。
　A：盲人按摩，我只听说过，但________没见过，我也从来没做过按摩。

3\. A：我是上网找到的。因为我想了解中国残疾人事业的情况。
　B：你________对残疾人事业这么关心？

4\. 因为我姐姐小时候，被汽车撞了一下，成了残疾人。________我对残疾人事业特别关心。

5\. 我学的特殊教育专业，毕业后，要________残疾人教育事业。

6. 我的朋友圈里，有不少这个专业的同学。认识她们以后，我________她们甘愿从事残疾人教育事业，可爱、可敬。
7. 我认识的残疾人，也一样可敬。就说给我按摩的盲人按摩师吧。她虽然是盲人，但非常善良，而且也非常专业。她对顾客的关爱，也________我感动。
8. 昨天她还对我说，不能太瘦了，为了健康，要增加营养。我听了心里暖暖的。一个盲人按摩师对顾客这么关爱，说明她有一________善良的心。

（四）**将 A、B 两列连线，组成正确对话，然后大声朗读** Match A with B to make correct dialogs and read them aloud

A	B
你做过按摩吗？	我还没去过，听说那儿很美。
你去过杭州吗？	浏览过是浏览过，但只是看看图片。
你吃过北京烤鸭吗？	来中国以后，我没得过病。
你爬过长城吗？	见过，我去动物园看的，特好玩儿。
你见过大熊猫吗？	吃过，很好吃。
你丢过东西吗？	没有，我很想去爬一爬。
你浏览过展览橱窗吗？	丢过，我丢过手机。
你来中国以后得过病吗？	我从来没做过。

（五）**选词填空并朗读下列句子** Choose the appropriate words to fill in the blanks, and read aloud the following sentences

因为……所以……　　　虽然……但是……

1. ________学校旁边 / 附近（fùjìn, around; nearby）就有超市，________买东西很方便。
2. ________他学得时间不长，________进步很快。
3. ________她住的地方离学校很远，________从来没迟到过。

4. 这次考试________不难，________我考得不太好。

5. ________早上来不及吃早饭，________不到中午就饿了。

6. ________今天天气不好，________我们不去公园了。

（六）你是 A，请你向 B 提问 Supposing you are A, ask B questions

1. A：________________________________？

B：你来电话时，我把手机调成了静音，没听见。

2. A：________________________________？

B：因为那时我正在工作，所以把手机调成了静音。

3. A：________________________________？

B：昨天我到一个养老院去做志愿者了。

4. A：________________________________？

B：是一个朋友介绍我去的。

5. A：________________________________？

B：我想为老人们做点儿事儿。

6. A：________________________________？

B：他们像我的爷爷奶奶一样，为他们服务我很快乐，而且他们还教我说汉语。

（七）根据实际情况回答问题 Answer the questions according to your actual situations

1. 昨天晚上八点多的时候，你在做什么呢？

2. 你以前知道按摩是怎么回事儿吗？

3. 你做过按摩吗？

4. 你想不想试试？

（八）和同学一起表演课文 Act out the text with your classmates

（九）读后说 Read the passage and say it

最近，我常去一个盲人按摩院按摩。因为我想了解中国残疾人事业的情况，就在网上找到了这个地方。

爱琳问我为什么对残疾人事业这么关心。说来让人难过，因为我姐姐就是残疾人。小时候，她被汽车撞了一下，成了残疾人。所以我非常了解残疾人，也非常同情他们。

为了从事残疾人事业，我考大学时考了特殊教育专业。当我知道中国这个大学有这个专业的时候，就决定休学一年，来中国留学。来到中国以后，我很快跟特殊教育专业的同学联系上了。现在我的微信朋友圈里有不少是特殊教育专业的同学。认识她们以后，我觉得她们甘愿从事残疾人教育事业，真是可爱、可敬。

我认识的一些残疾人也一样可敬。就说给我按摩的按摩师吧，虽然她是盲人，眼前都是黑暗，但心却一片光明。她很细心，也非常专业。每次她都一边给我按摩，一边跟我聊天儿。一次，她对我说："安丽啊，我想叫你安康（ānkāng, safe and healthy）。"我问："为什么？"她慢慢地说："一个人，一生平安、健康，就是最大的幸福啊！"我听了以后，半天没说话。

昨天，她又对我说："你不能太瘦了，凡事都有个度，过了就会出问题。为了健康，你要增加营养。"听了她的话，我心里暖暖的。一个盲人按摩师对顾客这么关爱，说明她有一颗善良的心！

（十）怎么表达 How to express

xǐhuan
喜欢（2） likes

Nǐ zuì xǐhuan zuò shénme?
1. A：你最喜欢做什么？
What do you like to do best?

Wǒ zuì xǐhuan dú shū.
B：我最喜欢读书。
I like reading best.

Nǐ juéde tā zhège rén zěnmeyàng? Nǐ xǐhuan tā ma?
2. A：你觉得她这个人怎么样？你喜欢她吗？

What do you think of her? Do you like her?

Wǒ juéde tā hěn kě'ài. Wǒ xǐhuan tā wēixiào de yàngzi, yě xǐhuan tā shuōhuà de yàngzi.
B：我觉得她很可爱。我喜欢她微笑的样子，也喜欢她说话的样子。

I think she's very lovely. I like her smile and I also like the way she speaks.

（十一）朗读中国经典诗词，请注意语音语调 Read aloud the classic Chinese poem and pay attention to the pronunciation and intonation

Cháng'é
嫦娥

[Táng] Lǐ Shāngyǐn
［唐］李商隐（813—858）

Yúnmǔ píngfēng zhú yǐng shēn, chánghé jiàn luò xiǎo xīng chén.
云母屏风烛影深，长河渐落晓星沉。

Cháng'é yīng huǐ tōu língyào, bì hǎi qīngtiān yèyè xīn.
嫦娥应悔偷灵药，碧海青天夜夜心。

（十二）请欣赏下列著名的词句 Please enjoy the following famous saying

Bù jīng yí shì, bù zhǎng yí zhì.
不经一事，不长一智。
A fall into the pit, a gain in your wit.

Dì-sìshí'èr kè Wǒ xiǎng bǎ tóufa rǎnchéng hēi de

第四十二课 我想把头发染成黑的

Lesson 42 I want to dye my hair black

一 课文 Text

（一）我要理个发

（在理发店）

A：我要理个发。

B：请您稍等一会儿。

A：好的。

（10多分钟后）

B：该您了。您要理什么样的？

A：修剪一下就行了，还保持原来的发型。

B：头发要分吗？

A：不用分。

B：剪短一点儿吧？

A：可以，但也不要剪得太短了。

B：好的。要不要刮脸和洗头？

A：要，再吹吹风吧。

B：知道了。您看这样行吗？

A：挺好的，理得不错。谢谢您！

B：不谢。

（二）我想把头发染成黑的

A：我想把头发染一下。

B：染成什么颜色的？

A：给我染成黑色的吧。

B：好的。

A：再把头发烫一下。

B：要不要做头部按摩？

A：这次不做了。

B：您看看怎么样？

A：很好，谢谢您！

B：不客气。

二 生词 New Words

1 染	rǎn	动	dye
2 理发	lǐ fà	动	have a haircut
理发店	lǐfàdiàn	名	barbershop
3 稍等	shāo děng		wait a minute
4 修剪	xiūjiǎn	动	trim
剪	jiǎn	动	cut; trim
5 保持	bǎochí	动	keep; maintain
6 发型	fàxíng	名	hair style
7 分	fēn	动	divide; part
8 短	duǎn	形	short
9 刮	guā	动	shave

10 吹风	chuī fēng	动	dry (one's) hair with a blower
吹	chuī	动	blow
11 黑色	hēisè	名	black
12 烫	tàng	动	have a perm
13 头部	tóubù	名	head

三 注释 Notes

"把"字句（2）

动词后边有"成、在、到、给"作结果补语，后边再带宾语时，要用"把"字句。

A "把" sentence is used if a verb is used together with "成，在，到，给" after it as a result complement and then followed by an object. For example:

1. 你想把头发染成什么颜色的？
   不能说：你想染头发成什么颜色的？
2. 我把大熊猫的照片发给我侄子了。
   不能说：我发大熊猫的照片给我侄子了。
3. 师傅已经把车开到楼下了。
   不能说：师傅已经开车到楼下了。
4. 你把这个小箱子放在座位上吧。
   不能说：你放这个小箱子在座位上吧。

四 练习 Exercises

（一）朗读下列发音相近的词语 Read aloud the following words with similar pronunciation

lǐ fà	lì fǎ	shāo děng	shǎo dòng
理发	立法	稍 等	少 动

xiūjiǎn 修剪	xiūjiàn 修建	xǐ tóu 洗头	xǐ shǒu 洗手
bǎochí 保持	bǎoshí 宝石	fàxíng 发型	fāxíng 发行

（二）替换并朗读 Replace and read aloud

1. 你要理成什么样的？

做	画	修
改	染	剪

2. 我想把头发 染一下。

衣服	洗	手机	修
语法	复习	生词	预习
练习	做	课文	翻译

3. 请给我把头发染成黑色的吧。

白	咖啡色	黄
红	这样	那样

4. 你要不要做头部按摩？

我们	去长城看看
你	去医院看看
咱们	问问老师
你	去劝劝她
这件事	告诉他
你	再学一年

（三）**选词填空并朗读下列句子** Choose the appropriate words to fill in the blanks and read aloud the following sentences

得　等　太　了　风

1. A：我要理个发。
   B：请您稍________一会儿。
2. A：该您________。您要理什么样的？
   B：修剪一下就行了，还保持原来的发型。
3. A：剪短一点儿吧？
   B：可以，但也不要剪得________短了。
4. A：要不要刮脸和洗头？
   B：要，再吹吹________吧。
5. A：您看这样行吗？
   B：挺好的，理________不错。

把　下　给　次　成

1. 我想把头发染一________。
2. 染________什么颜色的？
3. ________我染成黑色的吧。
4. 再________头发烫一下。
5. A：要不要做头部按摩？
   B：这________不做了。

（四）**将 A、B 两列连线，组成正确对话** Match A with B to make correct dialogs

A	B
你把作业做完了没有？	送给他女朋友了。
把这盆花放在哪儿呢？	放在这个包里了
你把车停在哪儿了？	翻译成西班牙语。
你想把这篇课文翻译成什么语？	放窗台上吧。
他把那件礼物送给谁了？	停在楼下了。
你把手机和钥匙放在哪儿了？	还没有呢。

（五）**根据实际情况回答问题** Answer the questions according to your actual situations

1. 你多长时间理一次发？
2. 你常去哪儿理发？
3. 你喜欢什么发型？
4. 你染 / 烫过头发吗？
5. 你做过头部按摩吗？

（六）**和同学一起表演课文** Act out the text with your classmates

（七）**读后说** Read the passage and say it

我的头发长了，快两个月没理了。所以，今天我去理发店理了个发。这个理发店就在我们学校旁边，离我住的公寓楼很近。理发师非常热情，工作也很认真。他问我要什么发型，我原来想剃个光头，可是朋友说我剃光头不好看。我就对理发师说："你随便吧，修剪一下就行，不要剪得太短了，还保持原来的发型。"他一会儿就剪好了，又给我洗了洗头、吹了吹风。我照了照镜子，显得精神多了。我向理发师表示感谢，我觉得他理得不错。

（八）**怎么表达** How to express

mǎnyì
满意　satisfaction

Nǐ zài zhèr shēnghuó de zěnmeyàng?
1. A：你 在 这儿 生活　得 怎么样？

How is your life here?

Hěn hǎo. Wǒ hěn mǎnyì.
B：很 好。我 很 满意。

Very good. I'm very satisfied.

Wǒ duì lǎoshī de jiàoxué fēicháng mǎnyì.
2. 我 对 老师 的 教学　非常　满意。

I'm very satisfied with my teacher's teaching.

（九）朗读中国经典诗词，请注意语音语调 Read aloud the classic Chinese poem and pay attention to the pronunciation and intonation

Wàng Dòngtíng
望　洞庭

[Táng] Liú Yǔxī
[唐] 刘 禹锡（772—842）

Hú guāng qiū yuè liǎng xiāng hé,　tán miàn wú fēng jìng wèi mó.
湖 光 秋月 两 相和，潭 面 无风 镜 未磨。
Yáo wàng Dòngtíng shānshuǐ cuì,　bái yín pán lǐ yì qīng luó.
遥 望 洞庭 山水 翠，白银盘里一青 螺。

（十）请欣赏下列著名的词句 Please enjoy the following famous saying

Yí cùn guāngyīn yí cùn jīn,　cùn jīn nán mǎi cùn guāngyīn.
一寸 光阴 一寸金，寸金 难 买 寸 光阴。

An inch of time is worth an inch of gold,
while an inch of gold can not buy an inch of time.

Dì-sìshísān kè　Zánmen qù tiàotiao wǔ ba

第四十三课　咱们去跳跳舞吧

Lesson 43　Let's go dancing

一　课文 Text

（一）咱们去跳跳舞吧

A：今天晚上礼堂有舞会，咱们去跳跳舞吧。

B：我可跳得不好。

A：跟我一起去吧。周末嘛，好好玩玩儿。

B：好吧。你喜欢跳什么舞？

A：我原来喜欢蹦迪，跳起来特带劲儿，是一种很好的娱乐。

B：现在呢？

A：现在我参加了一个舞蹈班，我们请了一位舞蹈学院的老师教我们。

B：一星期学几次？

A：老师只在周六来一次，我们差不多天天早上或下午跳。

B：老师教你们跳什么舞？

A：我跟她学会了几种少数民族的舞，觉得非常好。

B：哪些少数民族的舞？

A：有维吾尔族舞、蒙古族舞，还有藏族舞，舞姿都非常优美，非常好看。

B：听说中国的少数民族都能歌善舞。

A：是，他们的歌舞热情、奔放，激动人心。

（二）你跳得太好了

（在舞会上）

山本：兰笛，你给我们跳一个独舞吧。

兰笛：我跳一个刚学的吧，可能跳不好。

山本：我给你放音乐。

兰笛：谢谢你，山本！

山本：不客气。（兰笛跳完舞）兰笛，你跳得太好了，舞姿太美了。

兰笛：过奖了。这就是老师教我们的维吾尔族舞。

山本：真是美的享受。舞蹈的魅力就在于，它既能健身，又能陶冶情操。

兰笛：对！你说得太对了。

二 生词 New Words

1 跳舞	tiào wǔ	动	dance
2 礼堂	lǐtáng	名	auditorium
3 舞会	wǔhuì	名	ball; dancing party
4 蹦迪	bèng dí	动	go to discos
蹦	bèng	动	dance
迪＝迪斯科	dísīkē	名	disco
5 带劲儿	dàijìnr	形	interesting; exciting
6 娱乐	yúlè	名、动	entertainment; amuse
7 舞蹈	wǔdǎo	名	dance
8 学院	xuéyuàn	名	college
9 少数民族	shǎoshù mínzú		ethnic minority

	少数	shǎoshù	名	minority
	民族	mínzú	名	ethnic group
10	舞姿	wǔzī	名	dancing posture
11	优美	yōuměi	形	graceful
12	能歌善舞	nénggē-shànwǔ		good at singing and dancing
	歌舞	gēwǔ	动	singing and dancing
13	奔放	bēnfàng	形	bold and unrestrained
14	激动	jīdòng	动	excite
15	人心	rénxīn	名	feeling; heart
16	独舞	dúwǔ	名	solo dance
17	放音乐	fàng yīnyuè		play music
	音乐	yīnyuè	名	music
18	享受	xiǎngshòu	动	enjoy
19	魅力	mèilì	名	charm
20	健身	jiànshēn	动	keep fit
21	陶冶	táoyě	动	cultivate (one's taste)
22	情操	qíngcāo	名	sentiment

专名 Zhuānmíng Proper Nouns

1	维吾尔族	Wéiwú'ěrzú	Uygur ethnic group
2	蒙古族	Měnggǔzú	Mongolian ethnic group
3	藏族	Zàngzú	Zang (Tibetan) ethnic group

三 注释 Notes

（一）中国的民族

中国有 56 个民族。据最新一次人口普查，目前汉族人口约 12.86 亿，占总人口的 91.11%；少数民族人口约 1.25 亿，占总人口的 8.89%。

China is a country with 56 ethnic groups. The latest census shows that the population of Han ethnic group is about 1.286 billion, accounting for 91.11% of the total population of China, and the population of all the ethnic minorities is about 125 million, accounting for 8.89% of the total population.

（二）起来

"起来"用在动词或形容词后，表示动作或情况开始并持续。例如：

The "起来" is used after a verb or an adjective to indicate the beginning and continuation of an action. For example:

1. 她高兴得跳了起来。
2. 太阳升起来了。
3. 他一句话说得大家笑了起来。

四 练习 Exercises

（一）朗读下列发音相近的词语 Read aloud the following words with similar pronunciation

wǔhuì 舞会	wùhuì 误会	mèilì 魅力	měilì 美丽
wǔdǎo 舞蹈	wùdǎo 误导	mínzú 民族	mínzhǔ 民主
wǔzī 舞姿	wūzi 屋子	dúwǔ 独舞	dúwù 读物

（二）替换并朗读 Replace and read aloud

1. 咱们去跳跳舞吧。

唱唱歌　游游泳
散散步　打打拳
看看电影　听听音乐会

2. 我可跳得不好。

说　写　打　踢　弹　画

3. 你喜欢跳什么舞？

唱	歌	听	音乐
吃	菜	打	球
玩儿	游戏	表演	节目

4. 我参加了一个舞蹈班。

登山队　武术班　游泳队
书画班　合唱团　志愿者组织

5. 我们差不多天天跳。

练　唱　画　打　写　玩儿

6. 老师教你们跳什么舞？

做	题	唱	歌	打	拳
画	画儿	写	字	弹	琴

7. 你的舞跳得太好了。

汉语	说	歌儿	唱
汉字	写	画儿	画
琵琶	弹	太极拳	打

8. 现在，我已经学会了<u>几种中国少数民族的舞</u>。

用筷子吃饭	用汉语点菜
做中国菜	打太极拳
用汉语问路	网上购物
洗衣服	唱汉语歌

（三）**选词填空并朗读下列句子** Choose the appropriate words to fill in the blanks and read aloud the following sentences

跟　只　吧　会　特别

1. A：今天晚上礼堂有舞会，咱们去跳跳舞________。
   B：我可跳得不好。
2. A：________我一起去吧。周末嘛，好好玩玩儿。
   B：好吧，你喜欢跳什么舞？
3. 我原来喜欢蹦迪，跳起来________带劲儿，是一种很好的娱乐。现在我参加了一个舞蹈班，我们请了一位舞蹈学院的老师教我们。
4. A：一星期学几次？
   B：老师________在周六来一次，我们差不多天天早上或者下午跳。
5. 我跟她学________了几种中国少数民族的舞，我觉得非常好。

得　教　刚　情操　给　放

1. 兰笛，你________我们跳一个独舞吧。
2. 我跳一个________学的吧，可能跳不好。
3. 我给你________音乐。
4. 兰笛，你跳________太好了，舞姿太美了。
5. 你过奖了！这就是老师________我们的维吾尔族舞。
6. 舞蹈的魅力就在于，它既能健身，又能陶冶________。

想　笑　暖　刮　跳　叫

1. 那天，当我听到我拿到了来中国留学的奖学金，我高兴得________了起来。
2. 这个人我知道，可是我怎么也________不起来他的名字了。
3. 昨天刮了一天大风，今天又________了起来。
4. 看他摔倒在汽车前面，我吓得________了起来。
5. 他可有意思了，常常把我们逗得________起来。
6. 春天快到了，天气渐渐________起来了。

（四）跟同学一起练习下列会话 Practice the following conversation with your classmates

像亲人一样

A：这个假期你去哪儿了？

B：我去新疆旅行了，是一个维吾尔族同学邀请我去的。

A：是吗？怎么样？

B：我觉得少数民族真是热情好客。我到了他家，他们拿出很多好吃的给我吃，对我像亲人一样。

A：我和你的感觉一样。

B：你去哪儿了？

A：我去内蒙古了，住在一个蒙古族牧民家里。他们也准备了好多好吃的，还有一只烤全羊，我从来没有见过，更没有吃过。姑娘们还唱着歌跳着舞欢迎我们，那场面，我现在想起来还很感动。

B：要是有机会，我真想再去一次新疆。

A：我跟你想的一样，还想再去一次内蒙古。

小词典

亲人	qīnrén	名	one's family member

邀请	yāoqǐng	动	invite
好客	hàokè	形	hospitable
牧民	mùmín	名	herdman
烤全羊	kǎo quányáng		roast whole lamb
场面	chǎngmiàn	名	scene
机会	jīhuì	名	chance

（五）根据实际情况回答问题 Answer the questions according to your actual situations

1. 你会跳舞吗？
2. 你喜欢什么文艺（wényì, art and literature）活动？
3. 你是怎么过周末的？
4. 你和朋友常常做什么？
5. 现在你对什么最感兴趣？学会了什么？

（六）你是 A，请你向 B 提问 Supposing you are A, ask B questions

1. A：____________________？
   B：我参加了一个大学生环保志愿者组织。
2. A：____________________？
   B：我常常跟中国大学生一起活动。
3. A：____________________？
   B：我喜欢跟中国同学一起聊天儿。
4. A：____________________？
   B：我们互相帮助，我帮她 / 他练英语，她 / 他帮我练汉语。
5. A：____________________？
   B：我们相处得很好。
6. A：____________________？
   B：我每天都很快乐，大学生活特别有意思。

（七）和同学一起表演课文 Act out the text with your classmates

(八) 读后说 Read the passage and say it

我喜欢跳舞，还参加了一个舞蹈班，跟同学们一起学习中国少数民族的舞蹈。我们请了舞蹈学院的老师教我们，老师每周星期六来。我们差不多每天早晨或下午一起跳舞，我已经学会了维吾尔族舞和蒙古族舞。昨天晚上学校礼堂有舞会，我和朋友都去了，去的人真不少。我还给大家跳了一个刚学会的维吾尔族舞。山本说，她喜欢我的舞姿，我听了心里美滋滋的（měizīzī de, happy）。我觉得跳舞是一项很好的活动，既能健身又能陶冶情操，也使我的留学生活更丰富，更有意思。

(九) 怎么表达 How to express

kuàilè
快乐　happiness

Wǒ hěn kuàilè.
1. 我 很 快乐。

I'm so happy.

Tiào wǔ ràng wǒ xīnqíng yúkuài.
2. 跳 舞 让 我 心情 愉快。

Dancing puts me in a good mood.

Wǔdǎo néng ràng rén yóngyuǎn niánqīng.
3. 舞蹈 能 让 人 永远 年轻。

Dancing keeps people young forever.

(十) 朗读中国经典诗词，请注意语音语调 Read aloud the classic Chinese poem and pay attention to the pronunciation and intonation

Xiǎo Chí
小池

[Sòng] Yáng Wànlǐ
［宋］ 杨 万里（1127—1206）

Quányǎn wúshēng xī xì liú,　shùyīn zhào shuǐ ài qíng róu.
泉眼 无声 惜细流，树阴 照 水 爱 晴 柔。

Xiǎo hé cái lù jiānjiān jiǎo, zǎo yǒu qīngtíng lì shàng tóu.
小荷才露尖尖角，早有蜻蜓立上头。

（十一）**请欣赏下列著名的词句** Please enjoy the following famous saying

Péng shēng má zhōng, bù fú zì zhí.
蓬生麻中，不扶自直。

Bái shā zài niè, yǔ zhī jù hēi.
白沙在涅，与之俱黑。

When one is surrounded by the virtuous, he'll become upright himself.

When one falls in the ungraceful environment, he'll be as ungraceful as it.

Dì-sìshísì kè　　Zhèyàng de shìr shì nánmiǎn de

第四十四课　这样的事儿是难免的

Lesson 44　Such things are inevitable

一 课文 Text

（两个留学生在聊天儿）

A：时间过得真快呀，不知不觉来中国都半年了。

B：想家吗？

A：刚来时想，现在好多了。

B：我也是，刚来时很多地方都不习惯，因为连一句汉语都不会说、一个汉字都不认识、一个朋友也没有，我感到非常孤独和寂寞，所以特别想家。

A：我还常常遇到一些难堪的事儿，比如坐错车、走错路、说些连中国人都听不懂的汉语，这时就感到又紧张又不好意思。

B：我和你一样。不过，有时我也想，遇到这样的事儿是难免的。

A：你遇没遇到过让你感到难堪的事儿？

B：当然遇到过。那是刚来时，我去超市买东西，第一次扫码支付，怎么也搞不定。我一看后边儿排着好多人，就更紧张了，只好退到旁边儿。这时，一位老人用手机"嘀"的一声，把码一扫，付完款就走了。我看他像年轻人一样熟练，真是感到难堪。

A：后来呢？

B：我想，算了，不买了。这时，一个中国女孩儿看出了我的尴尬，就用英语说："需要帮助吗？"我看她亲切和善的样子，就不好意思地对她说："中国同学教过我，可是一紧张就忘了。"她笑着说没关系，就认真地、一步一步地告诉我怎么做。我按照她说的步骤，很快就搞定了。后来，我在校园里还碰到过这个女孩儿，原来她也是我们大学的同学。

A：我也有这样的经历呀。我第一次骑共享单车，用手机怎么扫，锁也打不开，急得出汗，也是一位不认识的中国同学帮我把车锁打开的。

B：来中国半年了，遇到不少新鲜事儿，长了不少见识，也交了不少朋友，让我感到了友谊的珍贵。我越来越觉得，来中国学汉语，是我人生最佳的选择。

A：我也是这样想的，汉语越学越让人着迷。

B：你这么一说，更增强了我学好汉语的决心和信心。我要珍惜来中国留学的这个好机会，继续努力，实现自己的梦想。

二 生词 New Words

1	难免	nánmiǎn	形	hard to avoid; inevitable
2	不知不觉	bùzhī-bùjué		unconsciously
3	连	lián	介	even
4	孤独	gūdú	形	lonely
5	寂寞	jìmò	形	lonesome; lonely
6	难堪	nánkān	形、动	embarrassed; embarrass

7	比如	bǐrú	动	take...as an example
8	紧张	jǐnzhāng	形	nervous
9	搞定	gǎo dìng	动	work out
10	排	pái	动	form (a line); line up
11	只好	zhǐhǎo	副	have to
12	退	tuì	动	retreat
13	嘀	dī	拟声	*an onomatopoeia for sound*
14	年轻	niánqīng	形	young
15	熟练	shúliàn	形	skillful; proficient
16	后来	hòulái	名	later; afterwards; then
17	女孩儿	nǚháir	名	girl
18	尴尬	gāngà	形	embarrassed
19	和善	héshàn	形	kind and gentle
20	步骤	bùzhòu	名	step
21	碰	pèng	动	meet; run into
22	经历	jīnglì	名、动	experience
23	共享	gòngxiǎng	动	share
24	单车	dānchē	名	bicycle
25	锁	suǒ	名	lock
26	打不开	dǎ bu kāi		cannot unlock
	打开	dǎ kāi	动	unlock
27	急	jí	形、动	worried; worry
28	新鲜	xīnxiān	形	fresh; new
29	友谊	yǒuyì	名	friendship
30	珍贵	zhēnguì	形	precious

31	越来越	yuè lái yuè		more and more
32	佳	jiā	形	good; fine
33	选择	xuǎnzé	动	choose
34	越……越……	yuè…yuè…		the more…the more…
35	着迷	zháo mí	动	be captivated; be fascinated
36	增强	zēngqiáng	动	enhance; strengthen
37	决心	juéxīn	名	determination
38	信心	xìnxīn	名	confidence
39	珍惜	zhēnxī	动	cherish; treasure
40	继续	jìxù	动	go on; continue
41	实现	shíxiàn	动	realize; come true

三 注释 Notes

（一）强调意义的表达：连……也 / 都……

汉语常用“连……也 / 都……”表示强调。介词“连”引出要强调的部分（一般是极端的情况），后边用“也、都”与之呼应。隐含有比较的语意，表示强调的对象尚且如此，其他的就更不用说了。例如：

In Chinese, “连……也/都……” is often used for emphasis. The preposition “连” introduces the part to be emphasized (usually an extreme case) and is followed by “也” or “都”. This structure implies a comparison, meaning “even the object for emphasis is like this, let alone the rest”. For example:

1. 刚来时，我连一句汉语都不会说。（多的更不会说了）
2. 来中国快半年了，她连北京也没去过。（别的地方更没去过了）
3. A：你读过这本书吗？
   B：没有，我连这本书的名字都没听说过。（更不可能读过）

4. A：你最近忙吗？

B：忙，常常连周六周日也不能休息。（平时更不能休息了）

(二) 越来越

“越来越”表示程度随时间的变化而变化。例如：

“越来越” means the degree changes over time. For example:

1. 这里一到六月，天气就越来越热了。
2. 我的汉语口语越来越好，所以我也越来越有信心了。
3. 我越来越喜欢打太极拳了。

(三) 越……越……

“越……越……”表示在程度上后一项随前一项的变化而变化。例如：

“越……越……” means in terms of degree, the latter one changes with the change of the former one. For example:

1. 你看，雪越下越大了，真好啊，我终于看到雪了。
2. 手机游戏越玩儿越入迷，最好少玩儿。
3. 虽然汉语越学越难，但我也越学越喜欢汉语了。

四 练习 Exercises

(一) 朗读下列发音相近的词语 Read aloud the following words with similar pronunciation

nánmiǎn 难免	nán mián 难 眠	nánkān 难堪	nánkàn 难看
xíguàn 习惯	xīguǎn 吸管	jǐnzhāng 紧张	jìn zhàng 进 账
yìsi 意思	yì sī 一丝	gǎndào 感到	gàndào 干道

（二）替换并朗读 Replace and read aloud

1. 时间过得真快呀，不知不觉来中国都半年了。

就到圣诞节了
又该过新年了
我都二十岁了
就该放寒假了
就快回国了

2. 我一看后边儿排着好多人，就更紧张了。

听到这个歌	很激动
紧张	忘了该说什么了
跟朋友聊天儿	聊半天
到星期六	去爬山
看见他	脸红

3. 我越来越觉得，来中国学汉语，是我人生最佳的选择。

有她这样的朋友真好
和各国的同学在一起学习真快乐
能上这样的大学很幸运
她 / 他对我像姐姐 / 哥哥一样亲切
来中国留学非常值得
遇到什么困难都不要怕

4. A：你觉得她 / 他怎么样？
   B：我觉得她 / 他又聪明又努力。

聪明	好学	温和	善良
亲切	热情	正直	真诚
认真	负责	大胆	心细

（三）**选词填空并朗读下列句子** Choose the appropriate words to fill in the blanks and read aloud the following sentences

感到　又　就　选择　开　着　多　实现

1. 时间过得真快呀，不知不觉来中国都半年了。我刚来时常常想家，现在好________了。
2. 我也是，刚来时很多地方都不习惯。因为不会说汉语，也没有朋友，所以________非常孤独和寂寞。
3. 我常常会遇到难堪的事儿，比如坐错车、走错路，说些连中国人都听不懂的汉语，这时就感到又紧张________不好意思。
4. A：你遇没遇到过让你感到难堪的事儿？

   B：当然遇到过。那是刚来时，我去超市买东西，第一次扫码支付，怎么也搞不定。我一看后边儿排着好多人，______更紧张了。
5. 我只好退到旁边儿。这时，一个中国女孩儿看出了我的尴尬，就用英语说："需要帮助吗？"我看她亲切和善的样子，就不好意思地对她说："中国同学教过我，可是一紧张就忘了。"她笑________说没关系，就认真地，一步一步地告诉我怎么做。我按照她说的步骤，很快就搞定了。后来，我在校园里还碰到过这个女孩儿，原来她也是我们大学的同学。
6. 我也有这样的经历呀。我第一次骑共享单车，用手机怎么扫，锁也打不________，急得出汗，也是一位不认识的中国同学帮我把车锁打开的。
7. 来中国半年多了，遇到不少新鲜事儿，长了不少见识，也交了不少朋友，让我感到了友谊的珍贵。我越来越觉得，来中国学汉语，是我人生最佳的________。
8. 你这么一说，更增强了我学好汉语的决心和信心。我要珍惜来中国留学的这个好机会，继续努力，________自己的梦想。

学　下　大　吃　想　快乐

1. 我喜欢吃中国菜，所以越________越胖了。
2. 我觉得汉语越________越有意思。
3. 雨越________越大了，看来今天去不成了。
4. 我越来越感到在这儿生活非常________。
5. 那天我差点儿没被车撞上，现在越________越后怕（hòupà, fear after the event）。
6. 我年龄越________越觉得时间的宝贵。

（四）将 A、B 两列连线，组成正确的句子，然后大声朗读 Match A with B to make correct sentences and read them aloud

1. "连……也 / 都……"

A	B
我连他的手机号	他连一天课都没落过。
这半年多	就去机场接朋友了。
这样的事儿我连听	我连一个字都还没写呢。
他连饭都没吃	都不知道，怎么跟他联系。
有些汉字	都没听说过。
今天的作业	连中国同学也不认识，我更不认识了。

2. "越来越"

A	B
十一月了，	就越来越觉得汉语有意思了。
我的汉语越来越好，	天气越来越冷了。
学会的生词和句子越来越多，	而我越来越胖了。
你来以后越来越瘦，	学习的信心也越来越足了。
来中国学汉语的外国人	越来越习惯了。
我对这里的生活	越来越多了。

3. “越……越……”

A	B
汉语越学越难，	越大，看来去不成公园了。
你看，雨越下	也越有意思。
这种东西越吃	就越贵，一分价钱一分货嘛。
东西越好，	越胖，你最好少吃。
留学这件事儿，我越想	越快，最后得了第一名。
他越跑	越感到幸运。

（五）**用“越来越”完成下列句子，然后大声朗读** Complete the following sentences with “越来越” and read them aloud

1. 冬天要来了，天气________________了。
2. 我的汉语说得________________了。
3. 我对这儿的生活________________了。
4. 我对中国社会________________了。
5. 现在我的朋友________________了。
6. 我的身体________________了。

（六）**跟同学一起完成并练习下列会话** Complete and practice the following conversations with your classmates

我是来学习的

（A 在接受记者 B 的采访）

A：你好！你是什么时候来中国的？

B：我是去年________月来的，来了________年多了。

A：你是从哪国来的？

B：我是从________来的。

A：你是一个人来的还是跟朋友一起来的？

B：我________来的。

A：你是怎么来的？

B：我坐________来的。

A：你是来旅行的还是工作的？

B：我不是来旅行的，也不是来工作的，我是来________的。

A：你汉语说得________。

B：马马虎虎（mǎmǎhūhū, just passable）吧，我的汉语带有________腔。

A：这是难免的。怎么样，一切都习惯了吧？

B：差不多吧，越来越习惯了。

A：谢谢你接受我的采访。

B：________。

（七）和同学一起表演课文 Act out the text with your classmates

（八）读后说 Read the passage and say it

时间过得真快，不知不觉来中国已经半年了。这半年，我遇到了不少事儿，有些事儿让我感到又尴尬又温暖。比如第一次去超市买东西，因为不会说汉语，听不懂营业员说的话，扫码支付的时候我怎么也搞不定。看到我后面排着很多人，我更加紧张，心想：算了，不买了。这时，一个中国女孩儿看出了我的尴尬。她从后面走到我身边，用英语对我说："需要帮助吗？"我看她亲切和善的样子，连忙向她表示感谢。我说："中国同学教过我，可是一紧张就忘了。"她笑着说没关系，然后就告诉我该怎么做。我按她说的步骤，很快就搞定了。

这个善良的女孩儿让我很感动。没想到，后来我在校园里又遇到了她，原来她也是我们大学的同学。

（九）怎么表达 How to express

kuājiǎng 夸奖	compliments

Tā zhēn shì gè hǎo gūniang.
1. 她 真 是个好 姑娘。

She's such a nice girl.

Tā wēnróu、qīnqiè yòu shànliáng.
2. 她 温柔、亲切 又 善良。

She is amiable and kind.

Tā shì nàme shànjiě-rényì.
3. 她 是 那么 善解 人意。

She is so understanding.

（十）朗读中国经典诗词，请注意语音语调 Read aloud the classic Chinese poem and pay attention to the pronunciation and intonation

Mù Jiāng Yín
暮 江 吟

[Táng] Bái Jūyì
［唐］白 居易（772—846）

Yí dào cányáng pū shuǐ zhōng, bàn jiāng sèsè bàn jiāng hóng.
一道 残阳 铺 水 中，半 江 瑟瑟 半 江 红。

Kělián Jiǔyuè chūsān yè, lù sì zhēn zhū yuè sì gōng.
可怜 九月 初三 夜，露 似 真 珠 月 似 弓。

（十一）请欣赏下列著名的词句 Please enjoy the following famous saying

Huā yǒu chóng kāi rì, rén wú zài shàonián.
花 有 重 开日，人 无 再 少年。

Flowers may bloom again, while a person will never be young again.

Dì-sìshíwǔ kè Jīntiān tiānqì zěnmeyàng

第四十五课 今天天气怎么样

Lesson 45 How is the weather today?

一 课文 Text

（一）今天天气怎么样

（早晨，丹尼丝和夏莲花在聊天儿）

夏莲花：几点了？

丹尼丝：都七点多了，该起床了。

夏莲花：我还想再睡一会儿。

丹尼丝：你怎么这么能睡呀？

夏莲花：我太困了。对了，今天你是不是又该去爬山了？

丹尼丝：是呀。

夏莲花：今天天气怎么样？

丹尼丝：天气预报说是晴天，最高温度22度，最低8度。秋季是收获的季节，也是这里最好的季节。天气不冷也不热，不怎么刮风也很少下雨。你们国家呢？

夏莲花：这儿一年有春夏秋冬四个季节，我们那儿跟这儿不一样，一年全是夏天。

丹尼丝：那多好啊！这样就可以常常去游泳，我也喜欢游泳。

夏莲花：可是没有红叶，也没有雪，我还是觉得太单调了。我盼着快点儿下雪，我好亲眼看看雪。

丹尼丝：等着吧，这儿一到冬天就会下雪。

夏莲花：那太好了！

（二）夏天是旱季

A：你对这儿的气候已经习惯了吧？

B：还不太习惯，太干燥了。这里的冬天特别冷，很少下雪，还常常刮大风，让人觉得很不舒服。你看我，皮肤也变粗糙了，嘴唇也常常干裂。

A：你们那儿冬天不冷吗？

B：是呀，冬天不冷，夏天也不热。不过，我们那儿的夏天是旱季，不怎么下雨，所以也很干燥。

A：夏天不下雨？

B：是。因为很少下雨，有些野外的花草树木，常常因为干旱而枯死，看着特别可怜。

A：那什么时候下雨呀？

B：冬季。我们那里冬季是雨季，常常下雨。

A：真有意思。

二 生词 New Words

1	天气	tiānqì	名	weather
2	预报	yùbào	名、动	forecast
3	晴天	qíngtiān	名	fine day
4	高	gāo	形	high; tall
5	温度	wēndù	名	temperature
6	度	dù	量	degree
7	收获	shōuhuò	动、名	gain; harvest
8	春季／天	chūnjì/tiān	名	spring
	夏季／天	xiàjì/tiān	名	summer

	秋季/天	qiūjì/tiān	名	autumn
	冬季/天	dōngjì/tiān	名	winter
9	季节	jìjié	名	season
10	冷	lěng	形	cold
11	雪	xuě	名	snow
12	单调	dāndiào	形	monotonous; dull
13	盼	pàn	动	hope for
14	气候	qìhòu	名	climate
15	干燥	gānzào	形	dry; arid
16	粗糙	cūcāo	形	rough
17	嘴唇	zuǐchún	名	lip
18	干裂	gānliè	动	crack
19	旱季	hànjì	名	dry season
	雨季	yǔjì	名	rainy season
20	野外	yěwài	名	open country
21	草	cǎo	名	grass
22	树木	shùmù	名	trees
23	枯	kū	形	withered
24	可怜	kělián	形、动	poor; pitiful; have pity on

专名 Zhuānmíng Proper Noun

夏莲花	Xià Liánhuā	name of a person

三 注释 Notes

（一）动词：好

动词“好”有“以便、可以”的意思，带动词宾语。例如：

The verb “ 好 ” means “in oder to; can”. It is usually followed by a verbal predicate. For example:

1. 我盼着快点儿下雪，好亲眼看看雪。
2. 带上这把伞吧，下雨好用。
3. 你留个电话吧，车修好以后好通知你。
4. 加上我的微信吧，有事儿好跟我联系。

（二）亲眼

“亲”表示“用自己的”。“亲眼看看”就是用自己的眼睛看看。“亲”还可以组成“亲口”“亲耳”“亲手”“亲身”“亲笔”等。例如：

“ 亲 ” means “with one’s own”, “ 亲眼看看 ” means “to see with one’s own eyes”. “ 亲 ” can also be used to make such words as “ 亲口 ” “ 亲耳 ” “ 亲手 ” “ 亲身 ”, etc. For example:

1. 我还没有见过雪呢，我希望早点儿下雪，好亲眼看看雪。
2. 这是她亲口对我说的。
3. 她送给你的生日礼物是她亲手做的。
4. 这件事儿是我亲耳听他说的。
5. 我去了一趟新疆，亲身感受到了少数民族的热情善良和好客。
6. 我们的校名是一位书法家亲笔题写的。

（三）怎么

1. 疑问代词“怎么”用于询问方式、方法、原因。例如：

The interrogative pronoun “ 怎么 ” is used to ask the way, method, or reason. For example:

（1）你是怎么学会弹琵琶的？

（2）你怎么那么怕冷？（怎么 = 为什么）

2. “怎么”用于表示程度时多用于否定式，如“不怎么”放在动词或形容词前面，表示“不太”“不大”“不常”的意思。例如：

“怎么” is usually used in negative form when it is used to indicate degree. For example, when “不怎么” comes before a verb or an adjective, it means “not very” or “not often”. For example:

（1）我们那儿夏天不怎么下雨，所以也很干燥。

（2）她的英语说得不怎么好，不过大概的意思我能明白。

四 练习 Exercises

（一）**朗读** Read aloud

1. 朗读下列发音相近的词语 Read aloud the following words with similar pronunciation

tiānqì 天气	xiánqì 嫌弃	jǐ diǎn 几点	jīdiàn 积淀
yùbào 预报	yībǎo 医保	wēndù 温度	wèn lù 问路
jìjié 季节	jǐ jié 几节	shōuhuò 收获	shòu huò 售货

2. 朗读下列短语和句子 Read the following phrases and sentences aloud

再睡一会儿　再读一遍　再听一遍　再去一次　再看一下

又去爬山了　又去跳舞了　又去超市了　又跟妈妈视频了

今天天气怎么样　爸爸的身体怎么样　你的学习怎么样

不冷也不热　不大也不小　不难也不容易　不贵也不便宜

不怎么刮风　不怎么下雪　不怎么喜欢　不怎么习惯

不怎么会写　不怎么会说

收获的季节　收获幸福　收获爱情　很有收获　努力就有收获

一到冬天就下雪　一到春天就开花　一到夏天就下雨

一到秋天树叶就红了

（二）替换并朗读 Replace and read aloud

1. 今天天气怎么样？

昨天比赛	最近身体
你的学习	爸爸工作
这次考得	山上的景色

2. A：几点了？
   B：都七点多了，该起床了。

七点半	吃早饭
快八点了	去教室上课
十二点	下课
十二点二十	吃午饭
四点多	去锻炼身体
十一点	睡觉

3. 你怎么这么能睡呀？

说	写	跑
玩儿	吃	喝

4. 太困了，我还想再睡一会儿。

美	拍一些照片
好喝	喝一杯
好吃	吃一个
好看	看一遍
好玩儿	玩儿一次

5. 你是不是又该去爬山了？

游泳	学琵琶	打太极拳
跳舞	上书法课	当志愿者

6. 现在是秋天了，天气凉快了。

冬天	冷
春天	暖和
夏天	热

（三）**选词填空并朗读下列句子** Choose the appropriate words to fill in the blanks and read aloud the following sentences

觉得　好　到　预报　就　季节　又　再

1. 她每天早上六点多________起床了。
2. 太困了，我还想________睡一会儿。
3. 对了，今天你是不是________该去爬山了？
4. 天气________说是晴天，最高温度 22 度，最低 8 度。
5. 这儿一年有春夏秋冬四个________，我们那儿跟这儿不一样，一年全是夏天。
6. 可是没有红叶，也没有雪，我还是________太单调了。
7. 我盼着快点儿下雪，我________亲眼看看雪。
8. 等着吧，这儿一________冬天就会下雪。

舒服　可怜　雨季　干燥　热　吧

1. A：你对这儿的气候已经习惯了________？
   B：还不太习惯，太干燥了。
2. 这里的冬天特别冷，很少下雪，还常常刮大风，让人觉得很不________。你看我，皮肤也变粗糙了，嘴唇也常常干裂。
3. A：你们那儿冬天不冷吗？
   B：冬天不冷，夏天也不________。不过，我们那儿的夏天是旱季，不怎么下雨，所以也很________。
4. 因为很少下雨，有些野外的花草树木，常常因为干旱而枯死，看着特别________。
5. 我们那里冬季是________，常常下雨。

收获　季节　预报　树木　盼　野外

1. 天气________也有不准的时候，说今天有雨，却是晴天。
2. 这半年我最大的________是交了几个好朋友。
3. 我最喜欢的________是秋季和春季。
4. 妈妈常常________我早点儿学成回国。
5. 我觉得城市绿化，既要有花草，更要有________。
6. 一到周末，我就想跟朋友开车到________去玩儿。

（四）和同学一起练习下列会话 Practice the following conversations with your classmates

1. A：这里秋天常刮风吗？
   B：秋天不怎么刮风也很少下雨。

2. A：他汉语说得怎么样？
   B：他说得还可以，就是声调不怎么准。

3. A：你们那儿冬天常下雪吗？
   B：我们那里冬天不怎么下雪。

4. A：口语课的课文你都能读吗？
   B：有的课文我不怎么会读。

5. A：她常玩儿游戏吗？
   B：因为要考试了，最近不怎么玩儿了。

（五）将 A、B 两列连线，组成正确的句子，然后朗读 Match A with B to make correct sentences and read them aloud

1.

A	B
要是你想学太极拳，	我想去旅行一次。
要是有时间，	我一定买最好的。
要是能在中国工作，	早上去，晚上就可以回来。
要是有钱，	我就把妹妹也接来学习。
要是可能，	就去体育馆报名吧。
要是坐高铁去，	我想工作两年再回国。

2.

A	B
一听见闹钟响，	你一看就看见了。
路上都是雪，特别滑，	就上床睡了。
昨天晚上我一洗完澡，	就看见来接我的爸爸妈妈了。
我一出机场，	老师一讲他就懂了。
我的包就在桌子上，	我就立刻起床。
他很聪明，	我一出门就摔了一跤。

（六）**完成下列句子并大声朗读** Complete the following sentences and read them aloud

1. 我____________，校长给我朋友戴上一枚荣誉奖章（róngyù jiǎngzhāng, medal of honor）。（亲眼）
2. 我住在中国人家里，____________。（亲身）
3. 我们大学的校名，是一位名人____________。（亲笔）
4. 这件毛衣是我来中国前，妈妈____________。（亲手）
5. 她____________，明年她还要继续在这里学习。（亲口）
6. 这件事别人不能代办（dàibàn, do something for someone），必须____________。（亲自）

（七）**完成下列会话并大声朗读** Complete the following conversations and read them aloud

1. A：____________？
   B：都七点多了，该起床了。
2. A：你怎么这么能睡呀？
   B：____________。
3. A：今天天气怎么样？
   B：____________。
   （晴天　最高　最低）
4. A：这儿的秋天怎么样？
   B：____________。
   （最　不……也不……　不怎么）

5. A：你们国家的天气怎么样？

B：________________________________。

（有　四个季节　不一样　全是）

6. A：一年都是夏天多好啊，可以常常去游泳啊。

B：________________________________。

（可是　也　单调）

7. A：你没有见过雪，对吧？

B：________________________________。

（所以　盼　亲眼）

8. A：________________________________。（一……就……）

B：那太好了。

（八）和同学一起表演课文 Act out the text with your classmates

（九）读后说 Read the passage and say it

1. 朗读 Read aloud

北京一年有春夏秋冬四个季节：三月、四月、五月是春季；六月、七月、八月是夏季；九月、十月、十一月是秋季；十二月、一月和二月是冬季。

现在是秋天，是一年中最好的季节。北京的秋天，天气不冷也不热，不刮风也很少下雨。秋天还有一个重阳节。重阳节是登高节，也是敬老节，每到这一天，年轻人都会陪着老人，高高兴兴地去登山望远，看红叶、赏美景。

冬天来了，天气冷了。北京的冬天不怎么下雪，所以只要一下雪，人们就会高高兴兴地到雪地里去拍雪景、堆雪人、打雪仗，孩子们在雪地上玩儿得不愿回家。有一句俗语“瑞雪兆丰年”，说的是只要冬天能下几次大雪，来年一定是好收成。

春天到了，花开了，树绿了，公园、田野、山间，到处都有踏青赏花的人们。看到那一张张灿烂的笑脸，就能感受到他们的生活是多么美好！

北京的夏天很热，最高气温有时能到四十度。不过，夏天下雨的时候温度比较低，人们会感到舒服一些。

小词典

堆雪人	duī xuěrén		make a snowman
打雪仗	dǎ xuězhàng		have a snowball fight
瑞雪兆丰年	ruìxuě zhào fēngnián		a timely heavy snow promises a good harvest
收成	shōucheng	名	harvest; crop
田野	tiányě	名	field
踏青	tàqīng	动	(when the grass has just turned green) have an outing in spring
赏花	shǎng huā	动	enjoy the beauty of flowers
多么	duōme	副	how

专名

重阳节	Chóngyáng Jié	Double Ninth Festival
登高节	Dēnggāo Jié	another name for "重阳节 (Double Ninth Festival)"
敬老节	Jìnglǎo Jié	another name for "重阳节 (Double Ninth Festival)"

2. 回答下列问题 Answer the following questions

（1）北京一年有几个季节？每个季节是哪几个月？

（2）北京的春夏秋冬分别是什么样子的？

（3）重阳节又叫什么？这一天中国人会做什么？

（4）北京的冬天冷吗？下雪的时候，北京人喜欢做什么？

（**提示：**不认识的词，请问百度 / 谷歌。）

(**Reminder:** Search on Baidu/Google for the words you don't know.)

3. 你是 A，请你向 B 提问 Supposing you are A, ask B questions

（1）A：________________________？

B：北京一年有春夏秋冬四个季节：三月、四月、五月是春季；六月、七月、八月是夏季；九月、十月、十一是秋季；十二月、一月和二月是冬季。

（2）A：________________________？

B：现在是秋天，是一年中最好的季节。天气不冷也不热，不刮风也很少下雨。

（3）A：________________________？

B：秋天还有一个重阳节。重阳节是登高节，也是敬老节，每到这一天，年轻人都会陪伴老人，高高兴兴地去登山望远，看红叶、赏美景。

（4）A：________________________？

B：北京的冬天不怎么下雪。

（5）A：________________________？

B：只要一下雪，人们就会高高兴兴地到雪地里去拍雪景、堆雪人、打雪仗，孩子们在雪地上玩儿得不愿回家。有一句俗语“瑞雪兆丰年”，说的是只要冬天能下几次大雪，来年一定是好收成。

（6）A：________________________？

B：春天到了，花开了，树绿了，公园、田野、山间，到处都有踏青赏花的人们。

4. 自由表达 Express yourself freely

（1）请和同学一起，说说天气。

（2）向同学介绍一下你们国家的气候。

（3）向同学介绍一下，在你们国家，各个季节人们通常会做什么。

（十）怎么表达 How to express

zìxìn
自信 self-confidence

Wǒ yǒu xìnxīn, wǒ yídìng huì chénggōng de.
1. 我有信心，我一定会成功的。

I'm confident that I will succeed.

Wǒ duì wèilái shífēn lèguān.
2. 我对未来十分乐观。

I'm very optimistic for the future.

Tā zìxìn zìjǐ néng yíng.
3. 她自信自己能赢。

She is confident that she will win.

（十一）朗读中国经典诗词，请注意语音语调 Read aloud the classic Chinese poem and pay attention to the pronunciation and intonation

Chūn Rì
春日

[Sòng] Zhū Xī
［宋］朱熹（1130—1200）

Shèng rì xún fāng Sì Shuǐ bīn, wúbiān guāngjǐng yìshí xīn.
胜日寻芳泗水滨，无边光景一时新。
Děngxián shídé dōngfēng miàn, wànzǐ-qiānhóng zǒng shì chūn.
等闲识得东风面，万紫千红总是春。

（十二）请欣赏下列著名的词句 Please enjoy the following famous saying

Liángyán yí jù sān dōng nuǎn, èyǔ shāng rén Liùyuè hán.
良言一句三冬暖，恶语伤人六月寒

Kind words make one feel warm,
while harsh words make one feel cold in hot summer.

Dì-sìshíliù kè　Wǒ jīntiān yǒu gè yuēhuì

第四十六课　我今天有个约会

Lesson 46　Today I have a date

一　课文 Text

罗兰：爱琳，你今天要去哪儿？

爱琳：我今天有个约会。

罗兰：约会？你有男朋友了？

爱琳：哈哈，不是啊，我是去跟一位老爷爷约会。

罗兰：老爷爷？跟一位老人约会干什么？

爱琳：这位老爷爷喜欢在一条河边儿钓鱼。我呢，喜欢跟他聊天儿、练口语。

罗兰：这个老人是干什么的？你要警惕坏人，可千万别上当受骗啊！

爱琳：不会的。这位老爷爷可好了，慈眉善目、亲切和善，一看就知道是个好人。

罗兰：你跟他是怎么认识的？

爱琳：我和他是在我们大使馆的一次招待会上认识的。他退休前，在中国驻西班牙大使馆工作，是个外交官。他的西班牙语说得别提多好了！每次去他那儿跟他交谈，我都会感到有很大的收获。

罗兰：是吗？怪不得你汉语进步得这么快，说得那么好！

爱琳：哪里，你说得太夸张了吧。

二 生词 New Words

1	约会	yuēhuì	动、名	go out (with sb.); date
2	位	wèi	量	*a measure word for people*
3	爷爷	yéye	名	*a respectful form of address for a man of the older generation*
4	河边儿	hé biānr		riverside
	河	hé	名	river
5	钓鱼	diàoyú	动	go fishing
6	练	liàn	动	practice
7	口语	kǒuyǔ	名	spoken language
8	警惕	jǐngtì	动	be vigilant
9	坏人	huàirén	名	evil-doer; villain
10	上当	shàng dàng	动	be fooled
11	受骗	shòu piàn	动	be deceived; be cheated
12	慈眉善目	címéi-shànmù		benevolent and kind countenance
13	大使馆	dàshǐguǎn	名	embassy
14	退休	tuì xiū	动	retire
15	驻	zhù	动	be stationed
16	外交官	wàijiāoguān	名	diplomat
17	别提	biétí	动	not to mention
18	交谈	jiāotán	动	talk; chat

专名 Zhuānmíng Proper Noun

西班牙语	Xībānyáyǔ	Spanish (language)

三 注释 Notes

（一）副词：可

1. 副词“可”用于祈使句，强调某种要求、劝告、希望等。常跟“要”“得（děi）”“能”“别”合用。“可”不重读。例如：

The adverb “可” can be used in imperative sentences to emphasize a certain request, advice and hope, etc. It is often be used in conjunction with “要”“得”“能” and “别”, and can be unstressed. For example:

（1）这事儿你可别告诉她，因为她知道了会伤心的。

（2）你可别把什么东西落下了。

（3）天冷了，可得多注意，不要感冒了。

2.“可”用在陈述句中，表示强调，有“很、非常”的意思。“可”要重读，表示强调的语气。例如：

When used in a declarative sentence, “可” indicates emphasis, meaning “very”. It should be accentuated. For example:

（1）她可亲切了，对谁都是不笑不说话。

（2）她男朋友长得可帅了，跟电影明星（míngxīng, star）一样。

（3）这种桃儿可甜了，你尝尝。

（二）别提……了

动词“别提”常常与“了”合用，用于口语，表示程度很高。例如：

The verb “别提” is often used in spoken Chinese in conjunction with “了”, to indicate the degree is very high. For example:

1. 杭州的风景别提多美了。

2. 哈尔滨的冬天别提多冷了。

3. 坐高铁去，别提多快多舒服了。

四 练习 Exercises

(一) 朗读 Read aloud

1. 朗读下列发音相近的词语 Read aloud the following words with similar pronunciation

yuēhuì 约会	yě huì 也会	hé biān 河边	hèdiàn 贺电
diào yú 钓鱼	diàolí 调离	kǒuyǔ 口语	kǒuyì 口译
qīnqiè 亲切	qīnqi 亲戚	héshàn 和善	héshān 河山

2. 朗读下列短语和句子 Read the following phrases and sentences aloud

跟他 / 她有个约会　跟男 / 女朋友约会　约会时间　约会地点

可好了　可善良了　可努力了　可忙了　可难了　可有意思了

提高警惕　警惕坏人　保持高度警惕

千万别上当受骗　别上他的当　我上当了

别提多好了　别提多努力了　别提多美了　别提多高兴了

怪不得说得那么好　怪不得写得那么好　怪不得唱得那么好

进步很大　进步很快　很有进步　大有进步

3. 朗读下列带“可”的句子 Read aloud the following sentences containing “可”

(1) 你可不要太大意，一定要把安全放在第一位。

(2) 我们学校就在西山的大学区，环境可好了。

(3) 你要开车，可千万不要喝酒啊。

(4) 她可善良了，把自己在国际（guójì, international）比赛中得的奖金捐（juān, donate）给了慈善机构。

(5) 你可来了，我等了快一个小时了，可把人急死了！

(6) 这可真是个好消息呀！

(7) 那个公园可大了！一天都逛不过来。

（二）**替换并朗读** Replace and read aloud

1. A：这个女孩子怎么样啊？
   B：别提多善良了。

聪明	漂亮	努力
有人缘儿	热情	亲切

2. A：她汉语说得怎么样？
   B：她汉语说得可好了！

流利	地道	棒
标准	熟练	不错

（三）**选词填空并朗读下列句子** Choose the appropriate words to fill in the blanks and read aloud the following sentences

就　男/女　这么　怎么　条　干

1. A：今天我有个约会。
   B：约会？你有________朋友了？
2. A：哈哈，不是啊，我是去跟一位老爷爷约会。
   B：老爷爷？跟一位老人约会________什么？
3. 这位老爷爷喜欢在一________河边儿钓鱼。我呢，喜欢跟他聊天儿，练口语。
4. A：这个老人是干什么的？你要警惕坏人，可千万别上当受骗啊！
   B：不会的。这位老爷爷可好了，慈眉善目、亲切和善，一看________知道是个好人。
5. A：你跟他是________认识的？
   B：我和他是在我们大使馆的一次招待会上认识的。他退休前，在中国驻西班牙大使馆工作，是个外交官。他的西班牙语说得别提多好了！
6. A：每次去他那儿跟他交谈，我都会感到有很大的收获。
   B：怪不得你汉语进步得________快，说得那么好！

有人缘儿　忙　快　紧张　难　寂寞　高兴　棒

1. 运动会那天，她跑得别提多________了。
2. 她性格好，乐于助人，在我们班别提多________了。
3. 不管刮风还是下雨，他都坚持天天锻炼，所以身体别提多________了。
4. 一到节假日，中国的铁路运输（tiělù yùnshū, railway transportation）别提多________了。
5. 听说妈妈要来中国，她别提多________了，
6. 我上课时特别怕老师提问，老师一提问，别提多________了。
7. 刚开始学汉语时，我连“你好”都不会说，别提多________了。
8. 那时，我连一个朋友都没有，别提多________了。

（四）**根据课文回答下列问题** Answer the following questions according to the text

1. 爱琳要去跟谁约会？
2. 爱琳为什么要跟他约会？
3. 他们是怎么认识的？
4. 爱琳觉得这个老爷爷怎么样？
5. 这个老爷爷退休前做什么工作？
6. 爱琳的汉语说得怎么样？

（五）**跟同学一起练习下面的会话** Practice the following conversation with your classmates

约会

A：喂，你好，我是马丁。
B：马丁，你好，有什么事儿吗？
A：星期六晚上你有空儿吗？
B：有空儿，怎么了？
A：我想请你去音乐厅听音乐会。
B：什么音乐会？

A：是世界经典（jīngdiǎn, classical）音乐作品演奏会（yǎnzòuhuì, concert）。

B：我正想听这场音乐会呢，有票吗？

A：有。

B：太好了，我上网都没买到票。

A：这是一个朋友送给我的。

B：几点开始？

A：七点半，我们六点半出发，坐地铁去。

B：在哪儿见面？

A：六点半在公寓楼前面，我等你，不见不散。

B：好，不见不散。

（六）和同学一起表演课文 Act out the text with your classmates

（七）自由表达 Express yourself freely

跟同学介绍一下你来中国后认识的一位朋友。你们是怎么认识的？说说你知道的他 / 她的情况。

（八）读后说 Read the passage and say it

1. 朗读 Read aloud

杯子还是被子

每次去李爷爷那儿，他和奶奶都会给我做好吃的，留我和他们一起吃饭。有一天在饭桌前，奶奶不停地给我夹菜，说这个是你李爷爷做的，那个是你李爷爷炒的，都很好吃。李爷爷就笑着说："爱琳啊，你多吃点儿，这是你奶奶做的，很好吃。"看到两位老人互相夸赞，非常恩爱，我很羡慕。

昨天，奶奶问我："爱琳，你跟你爷爷练口语练了快三个月了吧？"

我说："是，快三个月了。"

"你汉语说得越来越流利了，就是声调不怎么准。"

"汉语的声调对我来说，有点儿难。"

"不要紧，以后奶奶也陪你练。咱们再学点儿成语、谚语什么的。"

“谢谢奶奶。我一定努力学习。”

这时，李爷爷倒了两杯热水，递给李奶奶一杯，也递给我一杯。我忙说，谢谢爷爷。

爷爷说，不客气，就又去给自己倒水。

但是，我不习惯喝热水。在我们国家，人们从来不喝热水，于是我忙叫住他说：“爷爷，可不可以给我一个 bèizi（被子：quilt）？”

李爷爷一听，愣住了。我又说了一遍：“请给我一个 bèizi，好吗？”李奶奶一听也愣了。他们俩你看我，我看你。奶奶问：“爱琳啊，你们学校宿舍里没有被子吗？”

“不，不，是喝水的‘被子’。”

“哦——”爷爷松了一口气，笑着问我：“爱琳啊，你要的是喝水的杯子（bēizi, cup）吧？”

李奶奶也笑着说：“小爱琳啊，真是太可爱了！”

你看，又闹笑话了吧。对我们留学生来说，学好汉语，发音和声调都是特别重要的。

小词典

杯子	bēizi	名	cup
被子	bèizi	名	quilt
不停	bù tíng		ceaselessly
夹	jiā	动	pick up (food with one’s chopsticks)
夸赞	kuāzàn	动	praise
恩爱	ēn’ài	形	affectionate (couple)
不要紧	búyàojǐn	形	never mind
成语	chéngyǔ	名	idiom
谚语	yànyǔ	名	adage
什么的	shénmede	助	and so on

愣	lèng	动	be dumbfounded
哦	ò	叹	oh
松气	sōng qì	动	relieve; relax
闹笑话	nào xiàohua		make a fool of oneself
重要	zhòngyào	形	important

2. 回答下列问题 Answer the following questions

（1）两位老人对“我”怎么样？

（2）“我”为什么要杯子？

（3）“我”为什么闹了一个笑话？

（4）你有没有因为发音和声调不准闹过笑话？

3. 你是 A，请你向 B 提问 Supposing you are A, ask B questions

（1）A：________________________________？

B：每次去李爷爷那儿，他和奶奶都会给我做好吃的，留我和他们一起吃饭。

（2）A：________________________________？（羡慕）

B：看到两位老人互相夸赞，非常恩爱，我很羡慕。

（3）A：________________________________？

B：我跟李爷爷练口语快三个月了。

（4）A：________________________________？（问题）

B：我汉语说得越来越流利了，就是声调不怎么准。

（5）A：________________________________？

B：我不习惯喝热水。在我们国家，人们从来不喝热水。

（6）A：________________________________？

B：我想向李爷爷要个杯子，把热水晾（liàng, become cool or cooler）凉了再喝。

（7）A：________________________________？

B：我把“杯子”说成了“被子”，所以他们不明白。

（8）A：________________________________？

B：我想告诉同学们，对我们外国留学生来说，学好汉语，发音和声调都特别重要。

（九）怎么表达 How to express

zhuǎndá
转达 passing on (a message)

Qǐng dài wǒ xiàng nǐ de fùmǔ wèn hǎo.
1. 请 代 我 向 你的父母 问 好。

Please give my best wishes to your parents.

Qǐng xiàng tā zhuǎndá wǒ de wènhòu.
2. A：请 向 她 转达 我的 问候。

Please give her my regards.

Nǐ fàng xīn, wǒ yídìng bǎ nǐ de huà zhuǎndá gěi tā.
B：你 放 心，我一定 把你的话 转达 给她。

Please rest assured that I will tell her what you said.

（十）朗读中国经典诗词，请注意语音语调 Read aloud the classic Chinese poem and pay attention to the pronunciation and intonation

Jiǔyuè Jiǔ Rì Yì Shāndōng Xiōngdì
九月 九日忆 山东 兄弟

[Táng] Wáng Wéi
[唐] 王 维（701—761）

Dú zài yì xiāng wéi yì kè, měi féng jiājié bèi sī qīn.
独在异乡 为异客，每 逢 佳节倍思亲。

Yáo zhī xiōngdì dēng gāo chù, biàn chā zhūyú shǎo yì rén.
遥 知 兄弟 登 高 处，遍 插 茱萸 少 一 人。

（十一）请欣赏下列著名的词句 Please enjoy the following famous saying

Lù yáo zhī mǎ lì, rì jiǔ jiàn rénxīn.
路遥 知 马力，日久 见 人心。

Distance tests a horse's stamina, and time reveals a person's heart.

Dì-sìshíqī kè　Lái, wǒmen gān bēi
第四十七课　来，我们干杯
Lesson 47　Let's drink a toast!

一　课文 Text

（一）为我们班得第一名，干杯

（同学们高兴地聚会，庆贺我们班在汉语节目表演中，得了第一名）

服务员：先生，现在点菜吗？

爱德华：请稍等一会儿，我们的人还没到齐呢。

服务员：那请先用茶。

李英爱：谢谢！

（过了一会儿）

爱德华：服务员，点菜！来一个铁板牛肉、一个辣子鸡丁、一个糖醋鱼、一个红烧排骨，要不要再来一只烤鸭呀？

李英爱：当然要了，再来一个砂锅豆腐、一个西蓝花、一个香菇菜心吧，女同学爱吃青菜。

服务员：要什么饮料？

爱德华：来两瓶啤酒。

李英爱：我要一杯茶，罗兰呢？

罗　兰：我也要茶。

爱德华：够了吧，太多了吃不了，不够再要。

李英爱：（对服务员）请快点儿上菜。

服务员：好的，请稍等。

（服务员上菜后）

李英爱：哎呀，这个菜怎么这么咸！服务员，这个菜太咸了，请给换一下。

服务员：啊，对不起，我给你们换一下。

（服务员端上新菜）

服务员：请您尝尝，这个怎么样？

李英爱：好点儿了。

爱德华：来，我们干杯！为我们班得第一，干杯！

全　体：干杯！

（二）我无所谓

服务员：请问，几位？

麦　克：两位。

服务员：你们要点儿什么？

麦　克：（问玛丽）你想吃什么？

玛　丽：随便，吃什么都行，你点吧。

麦　克：还是你来点吧，你喜欢吃什么，就点什么吧。

玛　丽：我要个烧茄子，你也点一个吧。

麦　克：来个红烧排骨，再来个铁板牛肉和两碗米饭。你想喝点儿什么？

玛　丽：我无所谓，喝什么都行。

麦　克：那就给你来杯橙汁儿，我要一瓶冰镇的啤酒。

玛　丽：够了，不够再说。

麦　克：请快点儿上菜。

服务员：好的，请稍等。

二 生词 New Words

1	干杯	gān bēi	动	drink a toast; cheers
2	聚会	jùhuì	动	(of people) get together; go for a party
	聚	jù	动	(of people) get together
3	庆贺	qìnghè	动	celebrate
4	节目	jiémù	名	program
5	表演	biǎoyǎn	动、名	perform; act; show
6	得	dé	动	get; obtain; gain
7	齐	qí	形	all ready; in order
8	铁板	tiěbǎn	名	iron board
9	辣子鸡丁	làzi jīdīng		Sauteed Diced Chicken in Hot Pepper Sauce
10	糖醋鱼	tángcùyú		Sweet and Sour Fish
11	红烧	hóngshāo	动	braise; stew
12	排骨	páigǔ	名	(of pork, mutton, and beef) spare rib
13	烤鸭	kǎoyā	名	roast duck
14	砂锅	shāguō	名	casserole
15	豆腐	dòufu	名	tofu
16	西蓝花	xīlánhuā	名	brocoli
17	香菇	xiānggū	名	shiitake
18	青菜	qīngcài	名	green vegetables
19	饮料	yǐnliào	名	drink; sth. to drink
20	够	gòu	动、副	reach or be up to (a certain standard) quite, rather
21	咸	xián	形	salty

22 无所谓	wúsuǒwèi	动	do not matter
23 随便	suíbiàn	动、形	do as one pleases; at will
24 烧茄子	shāo qiézi		Stewed Eggplant
烧	shāo	动	stew
茄子	qiézi	名	eggplant
25 橙汁儿	chéngzhīr	名	orange juice
26 冰镇	bīngzhèn	动	cool by ice; iced
27 再说	zàishuō	动	put off until some time later

三 注释 Notes

(一) 请用茶

"用"也有"吃、喝"的意思,"用茶"的意思是"喝茶"。"请先用茶"是尊敬的说法,意思就是:请先喝茶。还可以说"请用餐""请用饭"等。

"用" also means "to eat or drink", and "用茶" means "to drink tea". "请先用茶" is a polite expression, which means "to have some tea first". You may also say "请用餐" "请用饭", etc.

(二) 随便

"随便"既是动词也是形容词,动词"随便"可以分开用,可以说"随你/他的便",表示让某人怎么方便就怎么做;形容词"随便"表示怎么方便就怎么做,不多考虑。例如:

"随便" is both a verb and an adjective. When used as a verb, "随便" can be used separately, such as "随你/他的便", which means "to let somebody do things as he/she pleases". When used as an adjective, "随便" means "to do whatever is convenient and not need to think much about it". For example:

1. 随便,我吃什么都行,你点吧。(动词)
2. 你去也可以,不去也无所谓,随便吧。(动词)
3. 他这个人说话比较随便,你不要在意。(形容词)

（三）无所谓

"无所谓"的意思是：不在乎，没关系。例如：

" 无所谓 " means "not to care", or "not to mind". For example:

1. A：你想喝点儿什么？

   B：我无所谓，喝什么都行。

2. 这个活动是自由参加，你去不去都无所谓。

3. 这件事对我来说无所谓。

4. 穿什么牌子的衣服无所谓，只要自己觉得舒服就行。

（四）再说

动词"再说"表示留待以后办理或考虑。例如：

The verb " 再说 " means "to deal with or consider later". For example:

1. 我个人的问题回国以后再说，留学期间不考虑。

2. 别着急，这事儿等你伤好了再说。

"不够再要"也是个紧缩句，意思是：如果菜不够的话，再要。

" 不够再要 " is also a compressed sentence which means "to ask for more food if you don't have enough".

四 练习 Exercises

（一）朗读 Read aloud

1. 朗读下列发音相近的词语 Read aloud the following words with similar pronunciation

gān bēi 干 杯	gānbèi 干贝	diǎn cài 点 菜	tiān cài 添 菜
qìnghè 庆贺	qǐng kè 请 客	yòng chá 用 茶	yòng chā 用 叉
yǐnliào 饮料	yìngyāo 应邀	suíbiàn 随便	shuǐ biān 水 边

2. 朗读下列短语和句子 Read the following phrases and sentences aloud

请稍等　请稍休息一会儿　这个稍大了点儿　稍后再说

人到齐了　人来齐了　菜上齐了　东西买齐了

红烧肉　红烧排骨　红烧鲤鱼　红烧黄鱼

咸不咸　有点儿咸　咸了点儿　太咸了

端茶　端饭　端水　端酒　端过来　端上来

尝一尝　尝尝好吃不好吃　尝尝好喝吗　尝过了

我无所谓　他无所谓　吃 / 喝什么都无所谓

随你的便　随便点吧　随便吃　随便谈谈　别太随便了

这事儿以后再说　明天再说　下次再说　过两天再说　回国再说

（二）**替换并朗读** Replace and read aloud

1. 为我们班得了第一，干杯！

为我们队得了冠军（guànjūn, champion）
为我们两国人民的友谊
为在座朋友们的健康
为你二十岁的生日

2. 服务员，点菜，
来一个铁板牛肉。

糖醋鱼　红烧排骨　烧茄子
糖醋排骨　香菇菜心

3. 哎呀，这个菜怎么这么咸！

辣　淡　酸　苦　甜

4. 您尝尝这个怎么样？

听听　看看　用用
试试　穿穿　戴戴

5. A：你想吃点儿什么？
B：随便。吃什么都行。

喝	来	要	看	听	玩儿

6. 你喜欢吃什么咱们就吃什么。

喜欢喝什么	喝什么
喜欢玩儿什么	玩儿什么
愿意去哪儿	去哪儿
想怎么去	怎么去
想怎么办	怎么办

（三）**选词填空并朗读下列句子** Choose the appropriate words to fill in the blanks and read aloud the following sentences

得	只	什么	齐	点	杯	为	爱

1. ________我们班得第一名，干杯！
2. 同学们高兴地聚会，庆贺我们班在汉语节目表演中，______了第一名。
3. 请稍等一会儿，我们的人还没到________呢。
4. 服务员，点菜！来一个铁板牛肉、一个辣子鸡丁、一个糖醋鱼、一个红烧排骨，要不要再来一________烤鸭呀？
5. 当然要了，再来一个砂锅豆腐、一个西蓝花、一个香菇菜心吧，女同学________吃青菜。
6. 还是你来________吧，你喜欢吃什么，就点什么吧。
7. 我无所谓，喝________都行。
8. 那就给你来________橙汁儿，我要一瓶冰镇的啤酒。

烤鸭	聚	随便	尝	庆贺	干杯	点菜	无所谓

1. 今天晚上我想请几个朋友________一________，你也来吧。
2. 你不是在这个饭店吃过吗？你来________吧。
3. 为________两国建交（jiàn jiāo, establish diplomatic relations）五十周年，明天大使馆有个招待会（zhāodàihuì, reception），想请您参加。

4. 为我们两国人民的友谊________！

5. 我常听中国朋友说，不到长城非好汉，不吃________很遗憾，来中国当然要吃烤鸭了。

6. 你________一下，这个菜怎么样？

7. 你想吃什么就要什么吧，我________，什么都可以。

8. 请大家________点儿，就像到自己家里一样。

（四）**完成下列句子并大声朗读** Complete the following sentences and read them aloud

1. 每天早上起床后，我 ________________，然后去食堂吃早饭。（先）

2. 晚上，我都是 ________________，然后再预习第二天的生词和课文。（先）

3. 我先在这个大学学习一年汉语，________________。（以后）

4. 这次考试 ________________，尤其是听力，好多地方我都听不懂。（够）

5. 你真 ________________，遇到这样两位可亲可敬的老人，他们待你那么好。（够）

6. 这里的冬天真 ________________，你看我穿了多少衣服。（够）

（五）**完成下列会话并大声朗读** Complete the following conversations and read them aloud

1. A：先生，现在点菜吗？
   B：________________________________。（等　没来齐）

2. A：请先用茶。
   B：________________________________。

3. A：为我们班得第一名，干杯！
   B：________________________________。

4. A：要什么饮料？
   B：________________________________。
   （啤酒 / 橙汁 / 茶）

5. A：服务员，这个菜太咸了。

B：________________________________。（换）

6. A：________________________________？（怎么样）

B：我尝了尝，很好吃。

7. A：________________________________？（什么）

B：随便，吃什么都行。

8. A：________________________________？（要　什么）

B：我无所谓，你就随便点吧。

（六）和同学一起表演课文 Act out the text with your classmates

（七）读后说 Read the passage and say it

1. 朗读 Read aloud

新的生活

我怎么也没想到有一天我会来到中国，在这片土地上生活。

前年10月，我丈夫突然接到公司通知，说要派他到中国来工作。刚听到这个消息时，我感到很为难。在一个人生地不熟，而且语言也不通的地方怎么生活呢？可是又一想，觉得这对我也是一个很好的机会。我可以利用这个机会学汉语，体验中国的生活。于是我下定决心，到中国以后一定要好好地生活，而且要让自己的生活更充实、更快乐。

去年3月，我和孩子们来到了北京。刚来的时候，异国他乡的生活让我感到很困难。第一次去市场买菜，由于紧张，我连简单的“多少钱”也说不出来。因为语言不通，只好天天待在家里，更多的是担心孩子们的学习。多亏楼下一位热心的中国老奶奶帮助我，我才慢慢熟悉了周围的环境。

我每天要安排孩子们学汉语，上午送他们去补习学校，下午请家教在家里辅导。学了5个月后，9月份孩子们转入国际学校开始正常上课，我也在家一边做家务一边自学汉语。孩子们很快适应了学校生活，跟同学们一起上课、聊天儿、玩儿，进步很快，汉语说得非常流利。而我的汉语却没有多大进步。这使我感到，要学好汉语，就得上学。于是我决定去大学学习汉语。从此我从家庭主妇变成了一名留学生。对我来说，重新当学生并不容易。每天早上我的时间都很紧张，5点半起床，手忙脚乱地准备早餐，吃完饭后，孩子们去上学，丈夫去上班，然后我才能去学校上课。

为了给孩子们做榜样，再忙再累我都坚持天天到校上课。跟年轻的同学一起，坐在宽敞明亮的教室里听老师讲课，我感到自己也变年轻了。但毕竟年龄大了，记忆力不如年轻人了。有些字看着认识，可写的时候，却写不出来，总是忘。但我有个办法，就是：笨鸟先飞。每次上课前，我都充分地预习：生词一遍又一遍地边读边记；课文跟着录音，一遍又一遍地朗读，直到能背下来。

我总是鼓励自己，总有一天我也能说一口漂亮的普通话，写一手漂亮的汉字。即使结果不是十分满意，但只要努力过，就不会后悔。

现在我在初级班学习，这个学期我坚持天天上课，一天课也没落，门门功课的考试成绩都在80分以上。明年我要升入中级班继续学习。我希望当我结束在中国的生活回国的时候，我的汉语能说得像中国人一样流利。那样，回国后我就能用汉语工作，当有中国人遇到困难时，我也能够帮助他。

我感谢我的丈夫，给了我这样一次机会，让我重新回到了学生时代；也感谢老师们，那么耐心地教我，让我过上了一种全新的生活，而且生活得如此充实、快乐。

小词典

为难	wéinán	形	embarrassed; awkward
人生地不熟	rén shēng dì bù shú		be unfamiliar with the place and people
体验	tǐyàn	动	learn through practice; experience
充实	chōngshí	形	fulfilling
异国他乡	yìguó-tāxiāng		foreign country; alien land
待	dāi	动	stay

多亏	duōkuī	动	thanks to
熟悉	shúxi	动	be familiar with
补习	bǔxí	动	take a make-up course
转	zhuǎn	动	transfer
家务	jiāwù	名	house work
主妇	zhǔfù	名	housewife
手忙脚乱	shǒumáng-jiǎoluàn		hurry-scurry
榜样	bǎngyàng	名	good example; model for others to follow
宽敞	kuānchang	形	roomy; spacious
毕竟	bìjìng	副	after all
记忆力	jìyìlì	名	memory
笨鸟先飞	bènniǎo-xiānfēi		clumsy birds must start flying before the rest; the slow need to start working early
背	bèi	动	recite
即使	jíshǐ	连	even; even if

2. 朗读下列问句并回答 Read aloud the following interrogative sentences and answer the questions

（1）请说说本文的作者是什么人？

（2）她是跟谁一起来中国的？

（3）刚来时，她遇到了什么困难？

（4）她为什么要到大学去学习汉语？

（5）她是怎么坚持学习的？学得怎么样？

（6）她给自己提出的学习目标是什么？你有没有自己的学习目标？

3. 复述这篇课文 Retell this text

（八）怎么表达 How to express

zhùhè
祝贺　congratulations

Wǒ huòdéle quán'é jiǎngxuéjīn.
1. A：我 获得了全额 奖学金。

I have been granted a full scholarship.

Zhùhè nǐ.
B：祝贺你。

Congratulations!

Gōngxǐ nǐ,　wǒ jiù zhīdào nǐ néng tōngguò kǎoshì.
2. 恭喜你，我就知道你能　通过 考试。

Congratulations! I believe you could pass the exam.

Zhùhè nǐmen yíngle zhè chǎng bǐsài.
3. 祝贺你们 赢了 这 场 比赛。

Congratulations on winning the game.

（九）朗读中国经典诗词，请注意语音语调 Read aloud the classic Chinese poem and pay attention to the pronunciation and intonation

Cǎi Lián Qǔ
采莲曲

[Táng] Wáng Chānglíng
［唐］ 王　昌龄　（？—756）

Héyè luóqún yí sè cái,　fúróng xiàng liǎn liǎngbiān kāi.
荷叶罗裙一色裁，芙蓉 向 脸 两边 开。
Luàn rù chí zhōng kànbújiàn,　wén gē shǐ jué yǒu rén lái.
乱 入 池 中　看不见，闻 歌始觉 有 人 来。

（十）请欣赏下列著名的词句 Please enjoy the following famous saying

Tiān xíng jiàn,　jūnzǐ yǐ zìqiáng-bùxī.
天 行 健，君子以 自强 不息。

As Heaven keeps vigor throngh movement,
a gentleman should unremittingly practice self-improvement.

Dì-sìshíbā kè Tā zhǎng de shénme yàngr
第四十八课 他长得什么样儿
Lesson 48 What does he look like?

一 课文 Text

（一）你自己进去找吧

（在展览馆门前，安娜跟其他人走散了……）

马丁：请问，你看没看见一个姑娘进去？

门卫：从这儿进去的人太多了，我没注意，长得什么样儿？

马丁：留着披肩发，蓝眼睛，个子高高的，一米七左右，背上背着一个包。

门卫：也是外国人吗？

马丁：对，是俄罗斯人。

门卫：是不是戴着一副黑边眼镜？

马丁：没有，她没戴眼镜。

门卫：穿什么衣服？

马丁：上身穿着一件红衬衫，下身是牛仔裤，头上戴了顶白帽子。

门卫：对不起，我没有印象，你还是自己进去找吧。

马丁：谢谢。

门卫：不客气。

（二）他长得什么样儿

（在下山的路上）

A：请问，看没看见一个小伙子从这儿过去？

B：他长得什么样儿？

A：大高个儿，身高大约有一米八左右，小平头，戴着一副墨镜。上身穿一件白色的T恤衫，下面是短裤。

B：看见了。

A：他往哪个方向去了？

B：从这儿下山去了。

A：大概多长时间了？

B：十多分钟了吧。

A：就他一个人吗？

B：对。

A：没错，就是他，我们也快点儿下去吧。谢谢您了。

B：不客气！

二 生词 New Words

1	散	sàn	动	become separate
2	姑娘	gūniang	名	girl
3	门卫	ménwèi	名	doorkeeper
4	留	liú	动	wear (hair)
5	披肩发	pījiānfà	名	shoulder length hair
6	眼睛	yǎnjing	名	eye
7	个子	gèzi	名	height; stature
8	米	mǐ	量	meter
9	左右	zuǒyòu	名	around; or so
10	背	bèi	名	back of the body

11	背	bēi	动	carry on the back
12	副	fù	量	(*a measure word*) set; pair
13	上身	shàngshēn	名	upper part of the body
	下身	xiàshēn	名	lower part of the body
14	红（色）	hóng (sè)	名	red
	白（色）	bái (sè)	名	white
15	衬衫	chènshān	名	shirt
16	牛仔裤	niúzǎikù	名	jeans
17	印象	yìnxiàng	名	impression
18	小伙子	xiǎohuǒzi	名	young fellow
19	大高个儿	dà gāo gèr		tall person
20	身高	shēngāo	名	(of a person) height
21	大约	dàyuē	副	about
22	平头	píngtóu	名	crew cut
23	墨镜	mòjìng	名	sunglasses
24	T恤衫	T xù shān	名	T-shirt
25	短裤	duǎnkù	名	shorts
26	方向	fāngxiàng	名	direction

专名 Zhuānmíng Proper Noun

俄罗斯	Éluósī	Russia

三 注释 Notes

（一）怎么询问和描述一个人的长相及穿着

怎么问：How to ask

1. 长得什么样儿？
2. 个子有多高？/个子高不高？
3. 上身穿的什么衣服？下身穿的什么？
4. 戴没戴帽子/眼镜/项链儿？

怎么描述：How to describe

1. 留着披肩发，蓝眼睛，个子高高的，一米七左右。
2. 大高个儿，身高大约有一米八左右，小平头，戴着一副墨镜。
3. 上身穿一件白色的T恤衫，下面是短裤。
4. 戴着一顶白帽子/一个项链儿。

（二）还是

"还是"表示经过比较或考虑后做出选择，"还是"后面是所选择的内容。句子含有商量和希望的语气。例如：

"还是" indicates making a choice after comparison or consideration. "还是" is followed by the choice. The sentence has a tone of consultation and hope. For example:

1. 你还是自己进去找吧。
2. 我们还是坐高铁去吧，可以看看路两边的风光。
3. 你还是先从一年级学起比较好。

"还是"还表示行为、动作或状态保持不变；仍然。例如：

"还是" also indicates a behavior, an action, or a state remains the same. It means "仍然". For example:

1. 天气预报说今天还是有雨，带上雨伞吧。
2. 她明年还是在这儿学习。
3. 我还是不太习惯这里的气候。
4. 我还是喜欢吃清淡（qīngdàn, light, not greasy or rich）的饭菜。

（三）多

数词“多”用在数量词后表示不确定的数目。例如：

“多” is used after a quantifier to indicate an uncertain number. For example:

1. A：大概等了多长时间了？

   B：三十多分钟了。

2. 她大概有二十多岁。
3. 我们大学的留学生有一万多。
4. 买辆汽车得十多万。

注意：“十多万”和“十万多”的意思不同。

十多万：十万到二十万之间，不超过二十万。

十万多：十万以上到十一万以下，不超过十一万。

四 练习 Exercises

（一）**朗读** Read aloud

1. 朗读下列发音相近的词语 Read aloud the following words with similar pronunciation

gūniang 姑娘	gūliang 估量	yǎnjing 眼睛	yǎnjìng 眼镜
gèzi 个子	gēzi 鸽子	yìnxiàng 印象	yǐngxiǎng 影响
shàngshēn 上身	shāng shén 伤　神	dàyuē 大约	dàlüè 大略

2. 朗读下列短语和句子 Read the following phrases and sentences aloud

走散了　会散了　云散了　雾散了　烟散了

留着披肩发　留着短发　留着小平头　留着小胡子

大约九点　大约一个星期　大约两年　大约两千元

戴着眼镜　戴着墨镜　戴着手表　戴戒指　戴耳环

戴耳机　戴项链

穿着羽绒服　穿着毛衣　穿着白衬衫　穿牛仔裤　穿短裤　穿短裙

（二）替换并朗读 Replace and read aloud

1. 你看没看见一个姑娘从这儿进去？

小伙子	老爷爷
老奶奶	小孩儿
外国人	

2. 她个子高高的，一米七左右。

一米六几	一米六七
大约一米七	

3. A：她戴没戴着眼镜？
   B：戴着呢 / 没戴。

帽子	项链儿
耳环	手套儿
戒指	

4. A：你带没带手机？
   B：带着呢。

喝的	吃的	包
伞	护照	钥匙

5. 上身穿着一件红羽绒服。

下身	穿	一条牛仔裤
他手里	拿	一张游览图
她	戴	一副墨镜
背上	背	一个小包
手里	打	一把伞
墙上	挂	一张画儿

6. 你还是<u>自己进去找吧</u>。

坐车去吧
买这件吧
用这本词典吧
去图书馆看书吧
跟我们一起去吧
去跳跳舞吧

7. A：大约多长时间了？
   B：<u>十多分钟</u>了吧。

二十多天	半个多月
一个多星期	一年多

8. 就<u>他一个人</u>吗？

一辆车	一张票
这么多钱	你们两个人
学一年	去一天

（三）**选词填空并朗读下列句子** Choose the appropriate words to fill in the blanks and read aloud the following sentences

得	着	从	背	散	往

1. 在展览馆门前，安娜跟其他人走________了。
2. A：请问，你看没看见一个姑娘进去？
   B：从这儿进去的人太多了，我没注意，长________什么样儿？
3. 留着披肩发，蓝眼睛，个子高高的，一米七左右。背上________着一个包。
4. 她是不是戴________一副黑边眼镜，上身穿着红色羽绒服，下身是牛仔裤，头上戴了一顶白帽子？
5. 请问，看没看见一个小伙子________这儿过去？他大高个儿，身高大约有一米八左右，小平头。上身穿一件白色的T恤衫，下面是短裤。

6. A：他________哪个方向去了？
   B：从这儿下山去了。

姑娘　还是　大约　左右　上　个子　戴　多

1. 我们是在展览会上走散的。我的手机又没电了，跟她联系不________，所以非常着急。
2. 她是一个聪明美丽的________，又非常善良，所以很有人缘儿。
3. A：她的________有多高？
   B：大约一米七左右。
4. 昨天晚上他________十点多才回来。
5. A：租一套一室一厅的房子得多少钱？
   B：我想最少得两千________元。
6. 那个穿牛仔裤，________眼镜的姑娘是不是她？
7. 我们________骑车去吧，那儿离学校不远。
8. 外国留学生一个班有二十个人________。

（四）完成下列句子并大声朗读 Complete the following sentences and read them aloud

1. 我每天绕操场跑十多圈，大约有________________。（公里）
2. 昨天看展览，给我们讲解的那位小姐________________，讲得非常清楚，声音也很好听。（大约　岁）
3. 你查一下，从这里到上海的高铁票，________________。（大约）
4. 我们大学的外国留学生________________，他们来自世界一百多个国家和地区。（大约　人）
5. 我们学校的美国留学生不多，我们班________________。（就）
6. 老师要我们坚持用中文写日记，写多写少都行，可我一次________________。（就　字　句子）

（五）**完成下列会话并大声朗读** Complete the following conversations and read them aloud

1. A：请问，你看没看见一个姑娘进去？
   B：________________________________。
2. A：她长得什么样？
   B：啊，____________________________。
   （大高个儿 / 瘦高个儿 / 矮个儿 / 大胖子）
3. A：是不是戴着眼镜？
   B：________________________________。
4. A：穿什么衣服？
   B：上身____________，下身____________。（穿着）
5. A：你看他往哪个方向 / 哪边走了？
   B：________________________________。
6. A：他走了大约多长时间了？
   B：________________________________。（十多分钟）

（六）**和同学一起表演课文** Act out the text with your classmates

（七）**自由表达** Express yourself freely

请你从手机里挑出一张朋友 / 同学 / 亲人的照片，用汉语给同学介绍一下他 / 她的相貌、身高、穿戴等。

（八）**读后说** Read the passage and say it

1. 朗读 Read aloud

善良的回应

她是一个普通的女大学生，当她知道妈妈生病住院以后，就想减轻家里的负担，希望利用暑假这两个月的时间去打工挣一点儿钱。

她到一家公司去找工作，经理看了她的简历，摇摇头，拒绝了。

女大学生收回自己的材料，准备离去。当她用手掌撑椅子站起来时，手被扎了一下，手心冒出了一颗红红的小血珠。原来椅子上有一个钉子露出了头。她见桌上有铜镇纸，就用它把钉子轻轻敲平，然后转身离去。几分钟后，那位经理派人把她追了回来，说她被聘用了。

她不解，忙问："是真的吗？"

经理面带微笑地说："是！如果我们不聘用你，那将是一个错误。"

女大学生没有因为被拒绝而感到不满。当她发现那颗露头的钉子有可能伤到别人时，想到的是把它砸平。她这一小小的善行，向人展示了她美好的心灵，当然会有善的回应。

小词典

普通	pǔtōng	形	common; ordinary
减轻	jiǎnqīng	动	lighten; relieve
负担	fùdān	名	burden
简历	jiǎnlì	名	resume; CV
拒绝	jùjué	动	refuse
手掌	shǒuzhǎng	名	palm
撑	chēng	动	prop up; support
冒	mào	动	ooze
血	xuè/xiě	名	blood
珠	zhū	名	bead
钉子	dīngzi	名	nail
露	lòu	动	show; appear
铜	tóng	名	copper
镇纸	zhènzhǐ	名	paperweight
敲	qiāo	动	beat; hit
转身	zhuǎn shēn	动	(of a person) turn round
聘用	pìnyòng	动	employ
不满	bùmǎn	形	be unhappy; be unsatisfied

伤	shāng	动	injure; hurt
展示	zhǎnshì	动	show; reveal
回应	huíyìng	动	answer

2. 朗读下列问句并回答 Read aloud the following interrogative sentences and answer the questions

（1）这个女大学生为什么想去打工？

（2）经理看了她的简历有什么反应？

（3）她的手为什么冒小血珠？

（4）她是怎么处理钉子的？

（5）经理为什么又聘用了她？

3. 你是 A，请你向 B 提问 Supposing you are A, ask B questions

（1）A：________________________？（她　为什么）

B：她妈妈生病住院了，她想减轻家里的负担，希望利用暑假这两个月的时间打工挣一点儿钱。

（2）A：________________________？（你　为什么）

B：因为我看她简历很一般，也没有工作经验，所以就拒绝了。

（3）A：________________________？（怎么）

B：被拒绝后，她就收回了自己的材料。用手掌撑椅子站起来时，手却被扎了一下，还冒出了小血珠。原来椅子上有一只钉子露出了头。

（4）A：________________________？（她　怎么）

B：她见桌上有铜镇纸就用它把钉子轻轻敲平，然后才转身离去。

（5）A：________________________？（你　怎么）

B：看到她这一举动，我连忙派人把她追了回来。对她说，她被聘用了。

（6）A：________________________？（你　为什么）

B：因为我觉得，如果我们不聘用她的话，那将是一个错误。

4. 复述这篇课文 Retell this text

（九）怎么表达 How to express

zhùfú zhùyuàn
祝福/祝愿 blessing; good wishes

Zhùfú nǐ!
1. 祝福你！
Best wishes to you!

Zhù nǐ wànshì-rúyì!
2. 祝你万事如意！
I wish you all the best!

Zhù nǐ mèngxiǎng chéng zhēn.
3. 祝你梦想成真。
I wish your dreams come true.

（十）朗读中国经典诗词，请注意语音语调 Read aloud the classic Chinese poem and pay attention to the pronunciation and intonation

Dēng Guànquè Lóu
登鹳鹊楼

[Táng] Wáng Zhīhuàn
[唐] 王之涣（688—742）

Bái rì yī shān jìn, Huáng Hé rù hǎi liú.
白日依山尽，黄河入海流。
Yù qióng qiān lǐ mù, gèng shàng yì céng lóu.
欲穷千里目，更上一层楼。

（十一）请欣赏下列著名的词句 Please enjoy the following famous saying

Jìng yǐ xiū shēn, jiǎn yǐ yǎng dé.
静以修身，俭以养德。

Quietude promotes learning, and frugality cultivates virtue.

词汇表 Vocabulary

A	哎哟	āiyō	叹	(*expressing astonishment, pain or pity*) ow	39
	安度	āndù	动	spend one's remaining years in comfort	33
	按摩	ànmó	动	massage	41
	按摩师	ànmóshī	名	massagist	41
	按摩院	ànmóyuàn	名	massage parlor	41
B	白（色）	bái (sè)	名	white	48
	办法	bànfǎ	名	way; method	34
	半夜	bànyè	名	midnight	38
	榜样	bǎngyàng	名	good example; model for others to follow	47
	包裹	bāoguǒ	名	parcel	40
	包装	bāozhuāng	动	wrap sth. up	40
	保持	bǎochí	动	keep; maintain	42
	抱	bào	动	hold or carry in the arms	34
	杯子	bēizi	名	cup	46
	背	bēi	动	carry on the back	48
	背	bèi	动	recite	47
	背	bèi	名	back of the body	48
	被	bèi	介	(*used in a passive sentence to introduce the agent*) by	39
	被子	bèizi	名	quilt	46
	奔放	bēnfàng	形	bold and unrestrained	43
	笨鸟先飞	bènniǎo- -xiānfēi		clumsy birds must start flying before the rest; the slow need to start working early	47

	蹦	bèng	动	dance	43
	蹦迪	bèng dí	动	go to discos	43
	比	bǐ	介、动	than	35
	比如	bǐrú	动	bake...as an example	44
	毕竟	bìjìng	副	after all	47
	毕业	bì yè	动	graduate	36
	表示	biǎoshì	动	express; show	38
	表演	biǎoyǎn	动、名	perform; act; show	47
	别提	biétí	动	not to mention	46
	冰镇	bīngzhèn	动	cool by ice; iced	47
	补习	bǔxí	动	take a make-up course	47
	不满	bùmǎn	形	be unhappy; be unsatisfied	48
	不停	bù tíng		ceaselessly	46
	不要紧	búyàojǐn	形	never mind	46
	不知不觉	bùzhī-bùjué		unconsciously	44
	步骤	bùzhòu	名	step	44
C	采访	cǎifǎng	动	interview	33
	参观	cānguān	动	visit	33
	残疾	cánjí	名	disability	41
	残疾人	cánjírén	名	the disabled; the handicapped	41
	草	cǎo	名	grass	45
	产生	chǎnshēng	动	engender	38
	场面	chǎngmiàn	名	scene	43
	车闸	chēzhá	名	brake	36
	衬衫	chènshān	名	shirt	48
	撑	chēng	动	prop up; support	48
	成家立业	chéngjiā-lìyè		get married and start one's career	33
	成语	chéngyǔ	名	idiom	46
	橙汁儿	chéngzhīr	名	orange juice	47

充实	chōngshí	形	fulfilling	47
出来	chū lái	动	*used after a verb to indicate the direction of motion from inside*	39
出租车	chūzūchē	名	taxi	37
除了	chúle	介	except	39
橱窗	chúchuāng	名	show window	39
吹	chuī	动	blow	42
吹风	chuī fēng	动	dry (one's) hair with a blower	42
春季／天	chūnjì/tiān	名	spring	45
纯洁	chúnjié	形	pure	38
慈眉善目	címéi-shànmù		benevolent and kind countenance	46
从事	cóngshì	动	work on; be occupied in	41
粗糙	cūcāo	形	rough	45

D

……的话	…dehuà	助	(*used at the end of a conditional clause*) if	35
搭乘	dāchéng	动	travel by (plane ship, car, etc.)	37
打不开	dǎ bu kāi		cannot unlock	44
打开	dǎ kāi	动	unlock	44
打雪仗	dǎ xuězhàng		have a snowball fight	45
大高个儿	dà gāo gèr		tall person	48
大后天	dàhòutiān	名	three days from now	40
大使馆	dàshǐguǎn	名	embassy	46
大约	dàyuē	副	about	48
待	dāi	动	stay	47
带劲儿	dàijìnr	形	interesting; exciting	43
袋	dài	名	bag	40
单	dān	名	list; bill	40
单车	dānchē	名	bicycle	44
单调	dāndiào	形	monotonous; dull	45
得	dé	动	get; obtain; gain	47

	恩爱	ēn'ài	形	affectionate (couple)	46
F	发	fā	动	get; send out	36
	发热	fā rè	动	get hot	36
	发型	fàxíng	名	hair style	42
	方向	fāngxiàng	名	direction	48
	放	fàng	动	put; place	37
	放音乐	fàng yīnyuè		play music	43
	分	fēn	量	*a measure word*	35
	分	fēn	动	divide; part	42
	付出	fùchū	动	pay; expend	33
	负担	fùdān	名	burden	48
	副	fù	量	(*a measure word*) set; pair	48
G	甘愿	gānyuàn	动	(be) willing (to do sth.)	41
	尴尬	gāngà	形	embarrassed	44
	感	gǎn	动	feel	38
	感到	gǎndào	动	feel	38
	感动	gǎndòng	动、形	move; moved	41
	感激	gǎnjī	动	feel grateful	38
	干杯	gān bēi	动	drink a toast; cheers	47
	干裂	gānliè	动	crack	45
	干燥	gānzào	形	dry; arid	45
	高	gāo	形	high; tall	45
	搞定	gǎo dìng	动	work out	44
	歌舞	gēwǔ	动	singing and dancing	43
	个子	gèzi	名	height; stature	48
	共享	gòngxiǎng	动	share	44
	够	gòu	动、副	reach or be up to (a certain standard); quite, rather	47
	孤独	gūdú	形	lonely	44

孤寡	gūguǎ	形	widowed	33
姑娘	gūniang	名	girl	48
鼓励	gǔlì	动	encourage	39
故乡	gùxiāng	名	hometown	33
顾客	gùkè	名	customer	41
刮	guā	动	shave	42
怪不得	guàibude	副	no wonder	33
关机	guān jī	动	switch off	36
光临	guānglín	动	presence	35
国情	guóqíng	名	national condition	38
H 孩子	háizi	名	child	34
憨态可掬	hāntài-kějū		charmingly naive	34
寒假	hánjià	名	winter vacation; winter holiday	33
旱季	hànjì	名	dry season	45
行	háng	名	profession; line of business	37
好评	hǎopíng	名	favorable comment	38
好客	hàokè	形	hospitable	43
合适	héshì	形	suitable	35
和善	héshàn	形	kind and gentle	44
河	hé	名	river	46
河边儿	hé biānr		riverside	46
黑色	hēisè	名	black	42
红（色）	hóng (sè)	名	red	48
红烧	hóngshāo	动	braise; stew	47
后备箱	hòubèixiāng	名	car boot	37
后来	hòulái	名	later; afterwards; then	44
后天	hòutiān	名	the day after tomorrow	40
化	huà	后缀	-ize; -ity	33
坏人	huàirén	名	evil-doer; villain	46

欢迎	huānyíng	动	welcome	34
换	huàn	动	exchange	35
回应	huíyìng	动	answer	48
火锅	huǒguō	名	hot pot	39
货	huò	名	goods	35
J 机场	jīchǎng	名	airport	37
机会	jīhuì	名	chance	43
肌肉	jīròu	名	muscle	41
激动	jīdòng	动	excite	43
即使	jíshǐ	连	even; even if	47
急	jí	形、动	worried; worry	44
记忆力	jìyìlì	名	memory	47
季节	jìjié	名	season	45
继续	jìxù	动	go on; continue	44
寄	jì	动	send	40
寂寞	jìmò	形	lonesome; lonely	44
佳	jiā	形	good; fine	44
家务	jiāwù	名	house work	47
夹	jiā	动	pick up (food with one's chopsticks)	46
价钱	jiàqián	名	price	35
减轻	jiǎnqīng	动	lighten; relieve	48
剪	jiǎn	动	cut; trim	42
简历	jiǎnlì	名	resume; CV	48
件	jiàn	量	*a measure word for clothing, furniture, luggage, etc.*	40
健康	jiànkāng	形	healthy	41
健身	jiànshēn	动	keep fit	43
僵硬	jiāngyìng	形	stiff; rigid	41

交谈	jiāotán	动	talk; chat	46
教育	jiàoyù	名、动	education; teach	41
接	jiē	动	answer; receive	41
节目	jiémù	名	program	47
紧张	jǐnzhāng	形	nervous	44
尽力	jìn lì	动	do all one can; try one's best	37
经历	jīnglì	名、动	experience	44
警惕	jǐngtì	动	be vigilant	46
静音	jìng yīn	动	mute	41
久	jiǔ	形	long	36
拒绝	jùjué	动	refuse	48
聚	jù	动	(of people) get together	47
聚会	jùhuì	动	(of people) get together; go for a party	47
决心	juéxīn	名	determination	44
K 开机	kāi jī	动	switch on	36
看见	kàn jiàn	动	see	34
看起来	kàn qǐlái		it looks	35
看样子	kàn yàngzi		it looks as if	38
烤全羊	kǎo quányáng		roast whole lamb	43
烤鸭	kǎoyā	名	roast duck	47
颗	kē	量	*a measure word for anything small and roundish*	38
可爱	kě'ài	形	lovely; cute	34
可怜	kělián	形、动	poor; pitiful; have pity on	45
口语	kǒuyǔ	名	spoken language	46
枯	kū	形	withered	45
夸赞	kuāzàn	动	praise	46
夸张	kuāzhāng	形	exaggerated	41
快件	kuàijiàn	名	express delivery luggage, goods or mail	40

	宽敞	kuānchang	形	roomy; spacious	47
L	落	là	动	leave behind; forget to bring	37
	辣子鸡丁	làzi jīdīng		Sauteed Diced Chicken in Hot Pepper Sauce	47
	来不及	láibují	动	it's too late (to do sth.); there's not enough time (to do sth.)	38
	来得及	láidejí	动	there's still time; be able to do sth. in time	38
	懒洋洋	lǎnyángyáng	形	lazy; languid; listless	34
	老化	lǎohuà	动	age; become older	36
	老龄化	lǎolínghuà		ageing (process); ageing trend	33
	了	liǎo	动	(*used in after a verbconjunction with* "得" *or* "不") can	40
	冷	lěng	形	cold	45
	愣	lèng	动	be dumbfounded	46
	礼堂	lǐtáng	名	auditorium	43
	理发	lǐ fà	动	have a haircut	42
	理发店	lǐfàdiàn	名	barbershop	42
	连	lián	介	even	44
	连…带…	lián…dài…		*indicating two actions almost taking place at the same time*	34
	连滚带爬	liángǔn-dàipá		roll and crawl	34
	练	liàn	动	practice	46
	灵	líng	形	easy to handle	36
	浏览	liúlǎn	动	glance over; browse	39
	留	liú	动	wear (hair)	48
	露	lòu	动	show; appear	48
	轮胎	lúntāi	名	tire	36
M	满足	mǎnzú	动	satisfy	34
	盲人	mángrén	名	blind person	41
	毛衣	máoyī	名	sweater	40
	冒	mào	动	ooze	48

碰	pèng	动	meet; run into	44
披肩发	pījiānfà	名	shoulder length hair	48
皮鞋	píxié	名	leather shoes	35
聘用	pìnyòng	动	employ	48
平	píng	形	flat	36
平安	píng'ān	形	safe	37
平头	píngtóu	名	crew cut	48
破	pò	动	(be) broken	36
普通	pǔtōng	形	common; ordinary	48
Q 齐	qí	形	all ready; in order	47
起来	qǐ lái	动	*used after a verb to indicate estimation or express an opinion*	35
气候	qìhòu	名	climate	45
千万	qiānwàn	副	must; be sure to	37
敲	qiāo	动	beat; hit	48
茄子	qiézi	名	eggplant	47
亲人	qīnrén	名	one's family member	43
亲眼	qīnyǎn	副	with one's own eyes	34
青菜	qīngcài	名	green vegetables	47
轻	qīng	形	gentle	38
情操	qíngcāo	名	sentiment	43
情况	qíngkuàng	名	situation; condition	33
晴天	qíngtiān	名	fine day	45
庆贺	qìnghè	动	celebrate	47
秋季 / 天	qiūjì/tiān	名	autumn	45
取	qǔ	动	get; take; fetch	36
R 染	rǎn	动	dye	42
热	rè	形	hot	36
热心	rèxīn	形	warm-hearted; enthusiastic	38

人生地不熟	rén shēng dì bù shú		be unfamiliar with the place and people	47
人心	rénxīn	名	feeling; heart	43
瑞雪兆丰年	ruìxuě zhào fēngnián		a timely heavy snow promises a good harvest	45
S				
撒	sā	动	leak	36
撒气	sā qì	动	leak; get a flat tire	36
散	sàn	动	become separate	48
扫码	sǎo mǎ	动	scan a QR code	36
扫（描）	sǎo (miáo)	动	scan	40
砂锅	shāguō	名	casserole	47
善良	shànliáng	形	kind-hearted	41
伤	shāng	动	injure; hurt	48
赏花	shǎng huā	动	enjoy the beauty of flowers	45
上当	shàng dàng	动	be fooled	46
上身	shàngshēn	名	upper part of the body	48
烧	shāo	动	stew	47
烧茄子	shāo qiézi		Stewed Eggplant	47
稍等	shāo děng		wait a minute	42
少数	shǎoshù	名	minority	43
少数民族	shǎoshù mínzú		ethnic minority	43
伸手	shēn shǒu	动	stretch out one's hand	38
身高	shēngāo	名	(of a person) height	48
什么的	shénmede	助	and so on	46
师傅	shīfu	名	*a polite title for one with accomplished skills usually in a trade or handicraft*	37
实习	shíxí	动	practice; do an internship	33
实现	shíxiàn	动	realize; come true	44
实在	shízài	副、形	really	36

事业	shìyè	名	career	41
收成	shōucheng	名	harvest; crop	45
收获	shōuhuò	动、名	gain; harvest	45
收件	shōujiàn	动	receive (a mail, parcel, etc.)	40
手忙脚乱	shǒumáng--jiǎoluàn		hurry-scurry	47
手掌	shǒuzhǎng	名	palm	48
受	shòu	动	receive	34
受骗	shòu piàn	动	be deceived; be cheated	46
瘦	shòu	形	thin	41
熟练	shúliàn	形	skillful; proficient	44
熟悉	shúxi	动	be familiar with	47
树木	shùmù	名	trees	45
漱	shù	动	gargle	39
漱嘴	shù zuǐ	动	gargle	39
双	shuāng	量	pair	35
说明	shuōmíng	动、名	explain; explanation	41
饲养员	sìyǎngyuán	名	feeder; breeder	34
松气	sōng qì	动	relieve; relax	46
塑料	sùliào	名	plastic	40
随便	suíbiàn	动、形	do as one pleases; at will	47
锁	suǒ	名	lock	44
T				
T恤衫	T xù shān	名	T-shirt	48
踏青	tàqīng	动	(when the grass has just turned green) have an outing in spring	45
胎	tāi	名	tire	36
糖醋鱼	tángcùyú		Sweet and Sour Fish	47
躺	tǎng	动	lie	34
烫	tàng	动	have a perm	42
趟	tang	量	*a measure word for trips to and fro*	34

陶冶	táoyě	动	cultivate (one's taste)	43
特殊	tèshū	形	special	41
疼	téng	形	pain; ache	39
体验	tǐyàn	动	learn through practice	47
天气	tiānqì	名	weather	45
田野	tiányě	名	field	45
调	tiáo	动	set	41
跳	tiào	动	jump	39
跳舞	tiào wǔ	动	dance	43
铁板	tiěbǎn	名	iron board	47
停	tíng	动	stop	37
同情	tóngqíng	动	sympathize	41
铜	tóng	名	copper	48
头部	tóubù	名	head	42
突然	tūrán	形	suddenly	39
吐	tù	动	vomit	39
退	tuì	动	retreat	44
退休	tuì xiū	动	retire	46

W

外交官	wàijiāoguān	名	diplomat	46
外卖	wàimài	名	take-out	38
外胎	wàitāi	名	outer tube	36
晚年	wǎnnián	名	old age; senectitude; one's later years	33
为难	wéinán	形	embarrassed; awkward	47
伟大	wěidà	形	great	33
为	wèi	介	for	38
位	wèi	名	place; position	37
位	wèi	量	*a measure word for people*	46
喂	wèi	叹	hello; hey	37
温度	wēndù	名	temperature	45

文章	wénzhāng	名	article	39
无论	wúlùn	连	whatever; regardless of	34
无所谓	wúsuǒwèi	动	do not matter	47
舞蹈	wǔdǎo	名	dance	43
舞会	wǔhuì	名	ball; dancing party	43
舞姿	wǔzī	名	dancing posture	43

X

西蓝花	xīlánhuā	名	brocoli	47
下	xià	动	*indicating the capacity for holding or containing sth.*	37
下身	xiàshēn	名	lower part of the body	48
吓	xià	动	frighten	39
夏季 / 天	xiàjì/tiān	名	summer	45
咸	xián	形	salty	47
香菇	xiānggū	名	shiitake	47
箱子	xiāngzi	名	suitcase	37
享受	xiǎngshòu	动	enjoy	43
消息	xiāoxi	名	news	39
小费	xiǎofèi	名	tip; gratuity	38
小伙子	xiǎohuǒzi	名	young fellow	48
小声	xiǎo shēng		in a low voice	38
心	xīn	名	heart; mind	38
心情	xīnqíng	名	state of mind	38
心愿	xīnyuàn	名	wish	34
新鲜	xīnxiān	形	fresh; new	44
信	xìn	动	believe	41
信心	xìnxīn	名	confidence	44
兴	xīng	动	prevail; be in vogue	38
行李	xíngli	名	luggage	37
兴趣	xìngqù	名	interest	38

修	xiū	动	repair; mend	36
修剪	xiūjiǎn	动	trim	42
蓄	xù	动	store up	36
蓄电池	xùdiànchí	名	accumulator; storage battery	36
选择	xuǎnzé	动	choose	44
学院	xuéyuàn	名	college	43
雪	xuě	名	snow	45
血	xuè/xiě	名	blood	48
Y				
颜色	yánsè	名	color	35
眼睛	yǎnjing	名	eye	48
谚语	yànyǔ	名	adage	46
养老	yǎng lǎo	动	(provide) elderly care	33
养老院	yǎnglǎoyuàn	名	nursing home; old people's home	33
样式	yàngshì	名	style design	35
样子	yàngzi	名	look; appearance	34
邀请	yāoqǐng	动	invite	43
爷爷	yéye	名	*a respectful form of address for a man of the older generation*	46
野外	yěwài	名	open country	45
医院	yīyuàn	名	hospital	39
一切	yíqiè	代	all; every; everything	38
以前	yǐqián	名	before	33
以外	yǐwài	名	other than	39
一分价钱一分货	yì fēn jiàqián yì fēn huò		you get what you pay for	35
异国他乡	yìguó-tāxiāng		foreign country; alien land	47
音乐	yīnyuè	名	music	43
饮料	yǐnliào	名	drink; sth. to drink	47
印象	yìnxiàng	名	impression	48

	营养	yíngyǎng	名	nutrition	41
	优美	yōuměi	形	graceful	43
	优盘	yōupán	名	USB flash drive	40
	游客	yóukè	名	visitor; tourist	34
	友谊	yǒuyì	名	friendship	44
	娱乐	yúlè	名、动	entertainment; amuse	43
	雨季	yǔjì	名	rainy season	45
	预报	yùbào	名、动	forecast	45
	原来	yuánlái	副、形	originally; as a matter of fact; original	33
	远大	yuǎndà	形	lofty	33
	约会	yuēhuì	动、名	go out (with sb.) date	46
	越……越……	yuè…yuè…		the more... the more...	44
	越来越	yuè lái yuè		more and more	44
Z	杂	zá	形	sundry; mixed	39
	再说	zàishuō	动	put off until some time later	47
	增加	zēngjiā	动	increase; add	41
	增强	zēngqiáng	动	enhance; strengthen	44
	扎	zhā	动	prick	36
	展出	zhǎnchū	动	exhibit	39
	展览	zhǎnlǎn	动	exhibit	39
	展示	zhǎnshì	动	show; reveal	48
	着急	zháo jí	形	worried	37
	着迷	zháo mí	动	be captivated; be fascinated	44
	照顾	zhàogù	动	take care of; look after	33
	珍贵	zhēnguì	形	precious	44
	珍惜	zhēnxī	动	cherish; treasure	44
	镇纸	zhènzhǐ	名	paperweight	48
	侄子	zhízi	名	nephew	34

只好	zhǐhǎo	副	have to	44
志愿者	zhìyuànzhě	名	volunteer	33
质量	zhìliàng	名	quality	35
中成药	zhōngchéng-yào	名	Chinese patent medicine	40
重要	zhòngyào	形	important	46
珠	zhū	名	bead	48
主妇	zhǔfù	名	housewife	47
住	zhù	动	(*used after a verb as complement*) firmly	34
驻	zhù	动	be stationed	46
祝	zhù	动	wish	37
转	zhuǎn	动	transfer	47
转身	zhuǎn shēn	动	(of a person) turn round	48
装	zhuāng	动	put in	40
撞	zhuàng	动	crash	41
自动	zìdòng	副、形	automatically; automatic	36
总	zǒng	副	always	38
嘴唇	zuǐchún	名	lip	45
左右	zuǒyòu	名	around; or so	48
作品	zuòpǐn	名	work	39
座位	zuòwèi	名	seat	37

专名 Proper Nouns

爱琳	Àilín	name of a person	41
重阳节	Chóngyáng Jié	Double Ninth Festival	45
登高节	Dēnggāo Jié	another name for "重阳节 (Double Ninth Festival)"	45
敦煌	Dūnhuáng	Dunhuang	33
俄罗斯	Éluósī	Russia	48
桂林	Guìlín	Guilin	33
哈尔滨	Hā'ěrbīn	Harbin	33
杭州	Hángzhōu	Hangzhou	33
敬老节	Jìnglǎo Jié	another name for "重阳节 (Double Ninth Festival)"	45
孔子	Kǒngzǐ	Confucius	33
昆明	Kūnmíng	Kunming	33
蒙古族	Měnggǔzú	Mongolian cthnic group	43
上海	Shànghǎi	Shanghai	33
苏州	Sūzhōu	Suzhou	33
泰山	Tài Shān	Mount Tai	33
维吾尔族	Wéiwú'ěrzú	Uygur ethnic group	43
西安	Xī'ān	Xi'an	33
西班牙语	Xībānyáyǔ	Spanish (language)	46
西藏	Xīzàng	Tibet	33
西山	Xī Shān	a mountain in Beijing	33
夏莲花	Xià Liánhuā	name of a person	45
藏族	Zàngzú	Zang (Tibetan) ethnic group	43